The History of Mount Ida

Troy New York's Historic Vista

Don Rittner

New Netherland Press
Schenectady, New York

Looking west towards downtown Troy from Mount Ida, circa 1909.

©2016 by Don Rittner

All Rights Reserved. No part of this publication may be reproduced or transmitted in any form or by and means, electronic or mechanical, except brief quotes extracted for the purpose of book reviews or similar articles, with the permission in writing from the author.

First American paperback edition 2016.
ISBN-10: 0-9624263-6-9
ISBN-13: 978-0-9624263-6-0

Table of Contents

Acknowledgements, iv

Dedication, vi

Introduction, vii

Chapter One: In The Beginning, 1
 The Wilson Years, 5
 The Heartt Brother Years, 8
 Phillip T. Heartt., 10
 Albert Pawling Heartt, 11
 The Henry Vail Years, 16
 David Thomas Vail, the Nephew, 20
 The Warren Years, 21

Chapter Two: The Call for a Public Park, 35

Chapter Three: The Public vs. The Chamber, 45

Chapter Four: The Rise and fall of Prospect Park, 87

 The beginning of Decline of Prospect Park, 148

Chapter Five: The Future of Prospect Park, 153
 The Pool, 154
 The Gatehouse, 156
 Winter Access, 156
 Observation Tower, 158
 Roads and Trails and Playgrounds, 158
 Education, 158
 Lighting and Safety, 159
 Beautification, 159
 Band Shell, 159
 Restore Cemetery, 159
 Fencing, 160
 Police Patrol,160
 Dismantle the Uncle Sam Pavilion, 160
 Carriage Rides, 161
 Connect Mt. Ida Falls, 161
 Sources, 163

Dedicated to

Justyna Kostek

*Czlowiek stworzony jest z milości i do milości.
esteś moim powietrzem.*

Introduction

Troy New York's Prospect Park, located on Mount Ida, is a relict of the last glacial episode in North America and has a unique history of private to public ownership during Troy's 200 years of existence. Named for its Greek forbearer Mount Ida has a commanding view of the Hudson Valley. Overlooking the flood plain of the Hudson River and with a view of 25 miles on a clear day, Mount Ida was the private repose of some of Troy's earliest settlers including the Wilson Brothers, Samuel and Ebenezer. Samuel went on to become "Uncle" Sam, the nation's iconic caricature.

Until the later 17th century and intrusions of Europeans, Troy was the home of the Mohicans. Later the area became the location of three Dutch farms belonging to the Albany based Dutch Vanderheyden families. After the successful laying out of Lansinburgh further north in 1770, the three Vanderheyden farmers decided to get into the game and began to convert their farms to building lots. The Yankee invasion from New England during the 1790s filled in those lots and Troy grew into an industrial giant during the following years.

That greatness has come to past. A city now with more than a third of the former population gone, the city has tried a number of times to jump start back into relevance. During the last 50 years, the city suffered as people and businesses moved out, factories closed and demolished, and a heavy dose of apathy set in. Some have claimed there is a new renaissance taking hold – after several others that failed – and perhaps it is true. Nevertheless, Troy has a great history to be proud of and 2016 represents its Bicentennial Year as an incorporated city.

Prospect Park at one time was the city's crown jewel. It was well fought for during the early 20th century when the city's park movement began. When the park opened in 1909 it was one of the most popular parks in the Capital District and with 10,000 people enjoying the park on a single day. More than 5000 children used the playgrounds in a single week in 1920.

With the economic decay of the city beginning in the 1940s, the city's parklands also took a beating. As an example, Beman Park, the city's first public park no longer has its fountain, or even bronze plaques, stolen from the stone monuments that use to hold them. Empty and underutilized this park is internationally famous as the place where the first Cambrian Era fossils were ever found.

This book is about the history of Prospect Park and it is hoped that it will stimulate a new interest in bringing the park back to life. As a young boy I swam in the pool, enjoyed the playground, and explored many a location on the hills of this superb piece of nature. The future youngsters of Troy should have the same privilege.

Don Rittner
2016

TOP: Looking at Troy to the north from Mount Ida. BOTTOM: Looking South. Circa 1909.

Chapter One
In The Beginning

Troy's Mount Ida, which rises 285 feet above the Hudson River, was always a spectacular climb with the rewards being more than 20 miles of visual beauty up and down the Hudson River Valley. It certainly must have been a welcome place of repose for Native Americans who lived in the area before the European invasion of the region in the 17th century.

Mount Ida is a large delta covered with lake silt and sand. It is an artifact from a time when the Hudson Valley was covered with water as a large glacial lake – Lake Albany – stretched from Newburgh to Glens Falls, a result of the last ice age some 50,000 years ago.

In 1824, the Gazetteer of the State of New York wrote this:

"Mount Ida, the river-hill in the rear, rises to a most commanding elevation, crowned by the mansion of Deacon [Philip] Heartt, from which there is a very extensive view of the Hudson, and adjacent country."

In 1833, James Stuart published "Three Years in North America," a journal of his stay. He visited Troy and here is what he

1984 US topographic map showing top elevation of Mt. Ida.

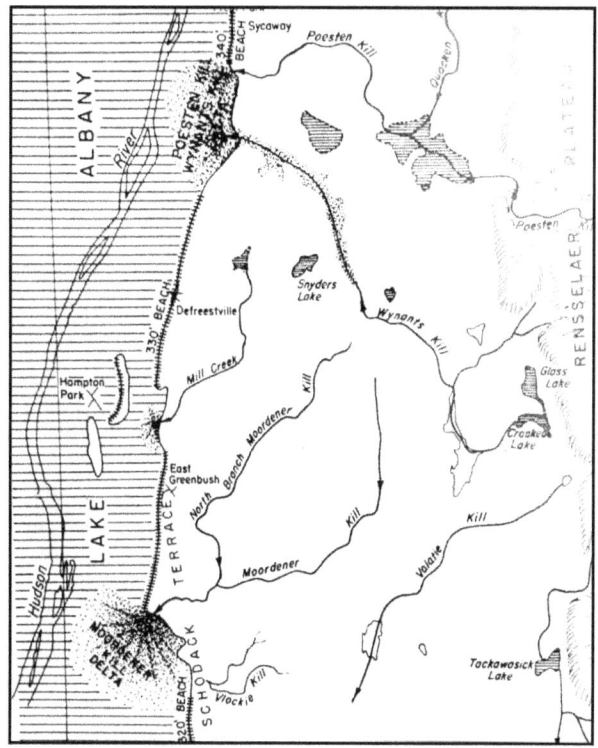

Mount Ida is the product of glacial activity over the last 10,000 years. The Poestenkill created a large delta into Glacial Lake Albany at the 350 foot above sea level mark. The lake clay are overlain with 25-40 feet of sand and gravel from the delta. Geology by Robert LaFleur.

W.H. Bartlett's view of Mt Ida in 1839. Looking south towards Albany.

wrote:

"About half-way up the hill called Mount Ida, we found a fence, and did not choose to invade it without permission. We therefore called at a cottage close to it, and found it occupied by a Scotch family, who had lately come to this country, and seem very happy. The name of the husband is William Craig, from Lochwinoch in Renfrewshire. His wife's name is Robertson. They arrived in the month of May 1828. Craig was, within a few days after his arrival, engaged by the proprietor of Mount Ida as a superintendent of his farm, at 170 dollars a year, besides a good house, the constant keeping of a cow,

1818 Map showing Ebenezer Wilson's Farm and farm of Philip Heartt.

vegetables, and potatoes. The proprietor was so much pleased with his management, that before the crop of 1829 was put into the ground, he insisted on Craig's becoming tenant of it. Craig in giving the proprietor the usual share of the produce, and the proprietor obliging himself, that if, according to this arrangement, Craig had not 170 dollars a year, besides the other articles before mentioned, he would make up the same to that amount."

In July 1837, a British Navy Officer Captain Frederick Marryat, C.B. and novelist visited Troy and wrote the following:

"Troy, like a modern academy, is classical, as well as commercial, having Mount Olympus on one side and Mount Ida in its rear. The panorama from the summit of the latter is splendid. I remained two hours perched upon the top of the mountain. I should not have staid so long, perhaps, had they not brought me a basket of cherries, so that I could gratify more senses than one. I felt becomingly classical whilst sitting on the precise birthplace of Jupiter, attended by Pomona, with Troy at my feet, and Mount Olympus in the distance."

In the popular book "American Scenery: or Land, Lake, and River Illustrations of Transatlantic Nature" by N.P. Willis in 1840, and in which W. H. Bartlett drew many scenes, here is what he says about Mount Ida:

"The scenery in this neighborhood is exceedingly beautiful. The junction of the Mohawk and Hudson, the Falls of Cohoes, the gay and elegant town of Troy, Albany in the distance, and a foreground of the finest mixture of the elements of landscape, compose a gratification to the eye equaled by few other spots in this country."

In the 1848 edition of "Horticulturist and Journal of Rural Art and Rural Taste, Volume 2," we find a plum unique to the area growing on Mt. Ida and named after the mount: The Ida Green Gage. Here is the discussion about it in the journal:

"The upper half of the Hudson River has, very deservedly, a high reputation for its plums. The heavy soil is peculiarly adapted to the growth and productiveness of this fruit, and there is scarcely a season when the fruit gardens and orchards, about Hudson, Albany, Troy (and we may include Schenectady,) do not offer a fine display of this excellent fruit.
The plum at the head of this article has considerable local reputation, as being a fine seedling fruit. Knowing our desire to examine specimens, Mr. Reagles, of Schenectady a nurseryman, who ranks it very high, had already propagated it to some extent, has very obligingly sent us specimens obtained from the original tree on Mount Ida, near Troy, NY accompanied by the following note:

"Schenectady, NY Sept 7"

"DEAR SIR – I send you, by express, specimens of the new seedling plum, called the Ida Gage, taken from the original tree now growing on Mount Ida, (Troy.). I am not aware yet to whom it owes its origin, but will endeavor to ascertain and inform you."
We presume this tree is a seedling of Mr. Heartt's in whose excellent fruit garden, on Mount Ida, we saw a number of seedlings resembling the green gage, some few years ago. – ep.

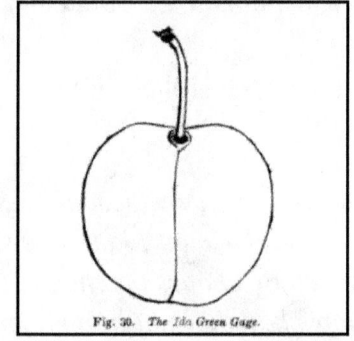
Fig. 30. *The Ida Green Gage.*

Regarding the qualities of the green gage, I have but to say, that it is equal to the green gage in flavor, superior to it in size and beauty, resembling a handsome red cheeked nectarine, to recommend it to fruit growers as worthy of a place in the smallest garden. I do not think I exaggerated its merits, taking every thing into consideration, when I say there is no plum extant superior to it. It is exquisitely beautiful, exceedingly luscious in flavor, productive, and hardy. You will, however, be best able to judge of its merits, and describe it, as I send you ripe specimens. Respectfully yours, C. Reagles Jr.

The editor of the journal adds his comments:

"A.J. Downing, Esq.

We are not willing to give any fruit so high a rank as our correspondent does the present one, without seeing it several seasons. We will, however, say that this is a most excellent seedling of the green gage, very strongly resembling it in flavor, and general appearance with the distinctive characteristic of larger size, a longer stalk and purplish red cheek, instead of the few streaks or dots of purple on the sunny side of the Green Gage.

It appears to be a distinct sub variety of the Green Gage, and if, as we are inclined to think likely from all we hear of it, it turns out to be uniformly larger and more productive, it will certainly take a high rank among plums.

As it is unquestionably the finest seedling fruit among a considerable number that we have examined this year, we shall describe it, and let another season's experience settle its exact merits. In the mean time, we think there can be little doubt, that it will prove a decided acquisition.

IDA GREEN GAGE*

Fruit roundish, strongly resembling the Green Gage in general appearance but one third larger. Suture very faintly marked half round. Skin of the colour of the Green Gage, but the sunny side washed with purplish red. Stalk nearly an inch long, rather slender, inserted in a very slight depression. Flesh greenish amber, very melting and juicy, separating freely from the stone, and

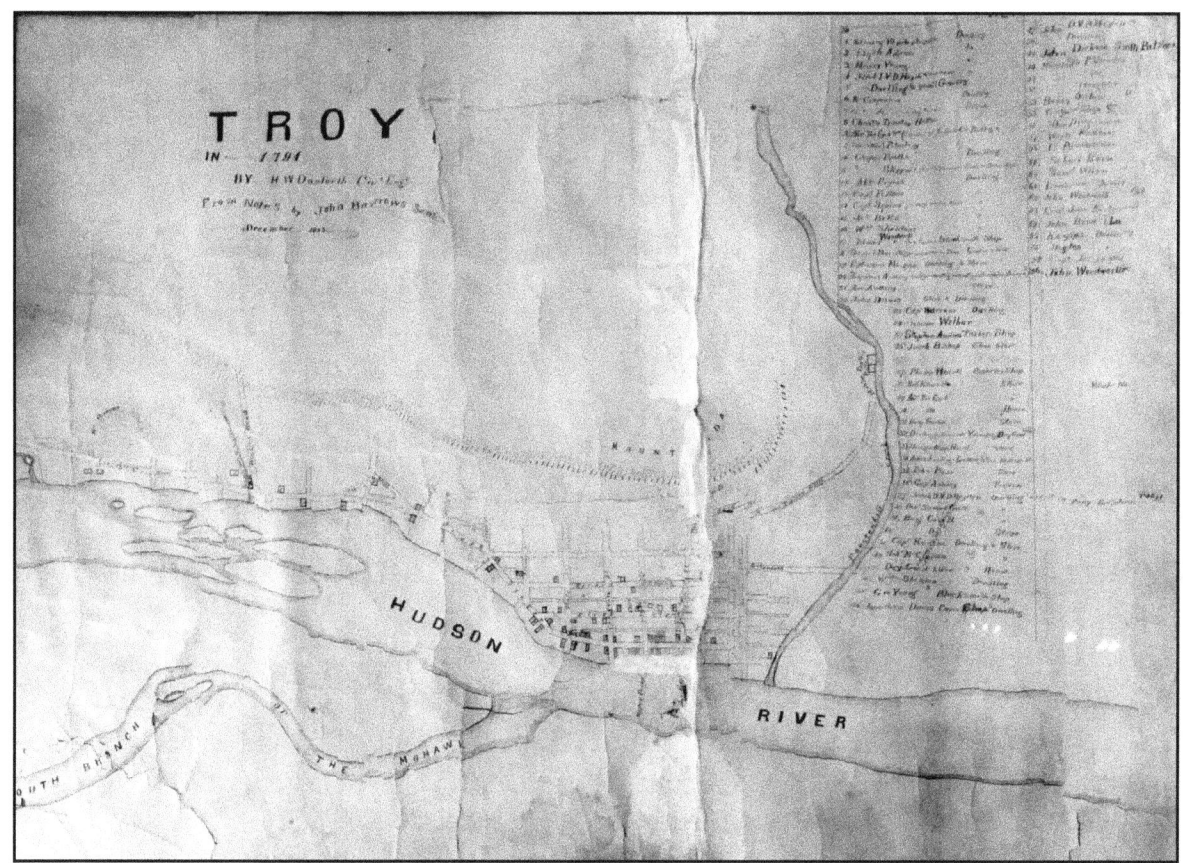

Map of Troy in 1791 Map shows what appears to be house on Mt. Ida that would have belonged to Ebenezer Wilson, Uncle Sam Wilson's brother.

of the sprightly luscious flavor of the old Green Gage. Stone small. It ripens about the same time with the Green Gage, or a few days later. Branches smooth, and the growth of the tree much like that of the Green Gage.

We propose to call this "Ida Green Gage," instead of simply "Ida Gage." to show the character; and that it is a sub variety, and not in all respects an entirely distinct sort."

The Green Gage was a synonym for the Reine Claude that was known for a longer time though nurseryman preferred using the Green Gage name. The American Pomological Society placed this variety of its fruit in their catalog of 1852. There was also a "Schenectady Catherine" grown for the record. Downing was editor of the Horticulturist and Journal of Rural Art and Rural Taste.

THE WILSON YEARS

When you speak of Samuel and Ebenezer Wilson, most of the discussion takes place about Sam, or "Uncle Sam" as he became known along with becoming the symbol of the United States during the 19th century (see my column http://blog.timesunion.com/rittner/will-the-real-uncle-

Troy from Watervliet in 1838 by W.J. Bennett. You can see a house on the top right on Mt. Ida. It may have belonged to Wilson or later the Heartt family.

sam-stand-up/3709/). Poor Ebenezer doesn't get as much attention but both boys came to Troy in its early days working together in slooping, brick making, meatpacking and other pursuits. It appears that the area known as Mount Ida was purchased either by both Wilson boys or Ebenezer shortly after they landed in Troy in 1789. While Sam lived in several houses downtown, his last one was on the side of Mount Ida on Ferry Street near Short 7th Avenue.

Ebenezer on the other hand had his house sitting directly on top of the hill overlooking the young city to be (Troy did not incorporate as a city until 1816). It is a bit more difficult finding any written history about Ebenezer that is not related to Sam.

We can assume that Ebenezer or brother Sam was the first to live on Mount Ida. A 1791 map of Troy shows what might appear to be a house site on Mount Ida. An 1818 map of Troy clearly has Ebenezer's house and gardens laid out with a road that begins on Congress as it passed Ferry Street and still exists today. It is called Cottage Road. The main house is flanked by four garden squares and behind to the east in an orchard with 35 trees. It also appears that a barn, or other outbuilding was adjacent to the orchard, which could have been worker quarters as well. There are no pictures of his house but it most likely was Federal or Greek Revival in style. A good clue is on a drawing of Troy from the Watervliet Arsenal by William James Bennet in 1838. The building seen on Mount Ida is not detailed enough but could be either Federal or Greek Revival from its generic appearance.

Troy from Watervliet in 1838 by W.J. Bennett. Closeup of house that may be part of the Wilson or Heartt estate on the top right on Mt. Ida.

Some of the earliest material found on Ebenezer starts in 1797 when he was appointed a meat packer of beef and pork in Troy. In 1802 he and Polly Mouton were married in Waterford. He was appointed a director of the Bank of Troy in 1813 and that same year the partnership of Wilson, Mann & Co, dissolved on September 28. That partnership started in 1810 with brother Samuel, James Mann, and himself selling dry goods, crockery and groceries. He and Sam were also in the slaughtering and packing business so perhaps he did not have time for both. During those years of the War of 1812 they established themselves as one of the best meat packers and of course led to their contracts with the government. By 1820 Ebenezer and his brother Andrew were starting a new slaughtering and packing firm in Albany near the river. Does that mean he and Sam were no longer working together? Around this time he was appointed inspector of beef and pork for the city and county of New York (1822, 1823) but it cannot be determined if he moved to New York City because in 1824 he was being appointed on a political committee in Troy. Unfortunately he died the following year on July 23, 1825. The New York Spectator wrote:

"Died Suddenly, yesterday after Mr. Ebenezer Wilson, Sen, aged 63. Mr. W. has for years been extensively engaged in business as an inspector and packer of beef, both in Troy, and this city (NYC). He was an ornament to the Christian church, and a worthy, industrious and excellent man in all the duties of life."

He appears to have had two sons Isiah M. and Ebenezer Junior who became a lawyer but there were ads in the local newspaper into the 1830s advertising the slaughtering business with the name Ebenezer Wilson as contact. His son may have dropped the junior since his father had died. A daughter Louisa Wilson Everngham lived in Brooklyn and in her obit in the New York Sun on November 20, 1889, we learn more about her than her father:

*"In her 93d Year
Death of Mrs. Everngham, who was born while Washington was President.
Mrs. Louisa Wilson Everngham died on Monday evening in her 93rd year, at the home of her daughter, Mrs. Henry Hawks, 117 Pacific Street, Brooklyn. She had preserved all her mental*

and physical faculties up to within a short time of her death. She always read the new books which made a stir in the world. And she had her own opinions of them. She read the newspapers every day. She especially admired Gladstone and Bismarck, and showed a surprising amount of knowledge in discussing their characters. She was an ardent Republican. The election of last year gave her especial pleasure. She was accustomed to take a turn around the block on pleasant days. And until a year or two ago she took these walks with a companion. Four weeks ago her health began to fail for the first time in many years, and she was obliged to take to her bed. Death resulted from a general breaking down of her system.

She was born in Troy before the expiration of the Washington Administration. Her father, Ebenezer Wilson, was one of that towns pioneer settlers and owned a large portion of its present site. When Miss Wilson was 27 years old her family moved to New York City, and she was married to Joseph Delaplaine Everngham, who afterward became one of New York's foremost merchants. He died in 1865. For the last thirty-five years Mrs. Everngham lived in the house where she died. She leaves four children, Mrs. Margaret Bell of Newburgh who is 70. William T. Everngham of Paterson, Mrs. M.H. Chapin, and Mrs. Henry Hawks. She had twelve living grandchildren. Two great grandchildren, and two great great grandchildren. She was a member of the Society of Friends, and was educated at the famous Nine Partners' Boarding School of the Quakers on the Hudson. The funeral will be held from the house on Thursday at 1 ½ o'clock."

In the NY Times obit about her it wrote: *"Ebenezer Wilson was an original settler and owner of Mount Ida. Now a populous district in the city itself."*

In summary it appears that Sam and Ebenezer (or just Sam) owned Mount Ida until 1820 when they sold all of it except for the four acres that Sam Wilson had his home on according to Sam Wilson's obit on August 2, 1854 in the Troy Daily Budget:

"Died. - Samuel Wilson, aged eighty-eight years, died this morning at his residence, 76 Ferry Street. The deceased was one of the oldest inhabitants of this city. He came to Troy about the year 1793, and consequently had resided here 61 years. He was about the last of those termed "first settlers," Mr. W. purchased the lands east of the city, now owned by Messrs. Vail and Warren, and occupied them for farming purposes till about 1820. He then sold them all, except about four acres, upon which his present residence stands. He has been one of the most active business men of the community, and we can say truly that he was an honest and upright man."

The Heartt Brother Years

Philip T. Heartt

Sometime before 1820, Sam Wilson sold half of Mount Ida to Philip Heartt. It is a fact that on the 1818 map of Troy, another large estate was located on the south end of Mount Ida and not far from the Wilson property with Heartt's name on it. This was the mansion of Philip Heartt, and it too was surrounded by artificial gardens and orchards and laid out very much in the A.J. Downing tradition (see maps 1818, 1845; Fig 42 in Downing's "Cottage Residences."). The road that extended from the Wilson property to Heartt entered a tree-lined driveway into a large oval garden divided into 8 plots. The house was surrounded by a neatly organized set of 16 trees, two rows of 8 each on the east side of the house. Behind the house were 16 rectangular garden plots and two orchards, one containing 25 trees and the larger one on the south side contained 70 trees! The Heartt mansion was built by journeyman carpenter Abram Nash and a partner named Chellus who came to Troy in 1804 and the only people living in the area, not a village yet, "was George Vail and Stephen Covell, according to Nash."

Philip T. Heartt came to Troy in 1790 and had a saddlery store on River Street, northwest corner of State and River Streets, with his brother Benjamin called P & B Heartt Hardware Merchants but it burned down on December 8, 1797 along with a house belonging to Asa Anthony. It was the burning down of Anthony's house that prompted the village of Troy to start a fire company and buy a fire engine in 1798. Nearby Lansingburgh had done the same that year and purchased a hand pump called "Old Black Joke" which you can see in the NY State Museum today.

The Heartt brothers built a new building on the site. Around 1805, he took on "Honest Ben Smith" forming Heartt & Smith, the "sign of the padlock" hanging over their door. They teamed up with Ebenezer Jones, Thomas Skelding, and Benjamin Highbee to start a crockery store called Jones, Smith & Co and took up the back of the store of Heartt & Smith with that one. It was Smith who gave a young Erastus Corning from Albany his first job at the store in 1807. Around 1812 the firm dissolved and later he formed P. Heartt & Sons. On June 20, 1820 that building burned and the warehouse across the street burned. They took up residence then near the northwest corner of River and Congress Streets in 1821 one door south of the post office. In 1827 that firm dissolved having as members Jonas C. Heartt, James Van Brackle, and Albert P. Heart. It then continued as J.C. Heart & Brothers made up of Jonas, Albert and Philip. Albert dropped out in 1840 or so and it became J.C. Heartt & Brother. The firm kept changing names and partners and by 1851 the only Heartt remaining was Charles S. Heartt. He and James H. Howe purchased the rights after Philip dropped out and continued at 181 River Street under the name Heartt & Co.

We know that by 1818 he built a farm on Mt. Ida next to Ebenezer Wilson, which you can clearly see on the 1818 map published by John Klein. This map is really the first map of the new city of Troy, incorporated only two years previous.

He did not confine himself to the hardware business. In 1839 he was a director of the Rensselaer and Saratoga Insurance Company and in 1851 one of the first directors with the creation of the Union National Bank at 12 First Street. In 1849, he was one of the heads of the George Washington Birthday celebration that took place in the Troy House. There were 13 regular toasts and 26 volunteer toasts after dinner! Some of the toasts were: " The Memory of Washington," "The President of the United States," "The President-elect, Zachary Taylor," "Our

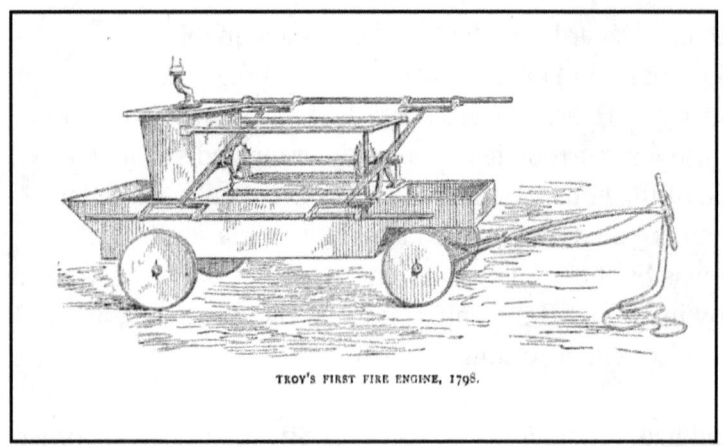

TROY'S FIRST FIRE ENGINE, 1798.

Ancient Ally, France," and "The Survivors of the Revolution." A special railroad car from the Troy & Greenbush Railroad waited for the Albany attendees to take them home. After all those toasts, it probably was a good idea.

His living arrangements according to the city directories is a bit scattered. In 1829 he is listed as living at 43 3rd Street and the following year at Mt. Ida, only to then get listed as boarding at the Troy House from 1831 to 39, with the exception of 1833 at the National House. Then in 1840 he is listed at 152 2nd St., followed by 8 Washington Place from 1841 to 1852 when he falls out of the directories altogether. The mansions on Mt Ida were called summer houses so it is likely he boarded in the city while working his various businesses and spent weekends at his summer house on Mt. Ida.

On December 14, 1855 Philip died. The Troy Budget published the following obituary:

"Death of PHILIP HEARTT. - Deacon Philip Heartt died in this city yesterday, in the 88th year of his age. He was born in Dutchess County in 1766. He was probably the oldest resident of Troy, having settled here in 1787, before the farms, which constitute the site of the compact portion of the city, were staked off in village lots. From that time to this he was closely and prominently identified with the interest of the place, and largely aided it through every state of its progress from an insignificant to a thriving and wealthy city of 35,000 inhabitants.

He commenced business in the village as a hardware merchant, and continued it for about thirty years, when he transferred it to his sons. He was a man of great industry and energy, which properly directed long since secured him a competence, and an enviable reputation among honorable business men."

One paper said *"He lived to 86 in full health but died from the effects of a shower bath taken in December 1863 to his fixed habits."* It appears that he probably took a fall in the shower?

At some time during his lifetime, he sold or bequeathed his Mt. Ida estate over to his brother Albert Pawling Heartt but we know A.P. was using the Ida Hill address

```
may 29                          E. WATERS, Jr.
NOTICE.—The co-partnership, formerly ex-
   isting between Jonas Coe Heartt, Albert P.
Heartt and Philip T. Heartt, under the firm of
Jonas C. Heartt and Brothers, has been dissolved
by the withdrawal of Albert P. Heartt from the
concern, by the mutual consent of all its mem-
bers. All persons indebted are hereby notified
that the subscribers only are authorised to settle
and receive the debts due to the firm, and to trans-
act all business relating to the former copartnership.
Dated Troy, May 27, 1839.
                           JONAS C. HEARTT,
may 29                     PHIL. T. HEARTT.
```

as early as 1843 and then 50 Second Street until 1851 when he is no longer listed in the city directories. He may have been living with his brother then at Ida Hill.

Albert Pawling Heartt

Albert P. Heartt is known for a number of things. First, he was the very first Trojan to build a house in the newly created Washington Park, the exclusive private park that was planned in 1840. It was a Greek Revival Townhouse at 171 Second Street that is still there.

In 1818, Heartt was one of the founding members, along with other locals and intellectuals of the time of perhaps the first natural history lyceum in the country - The Troy Lyceum of Natural History. **His first wife Susan C. Bayeux (1802-1825) was buried in the now bulldozed Mount Ida Burying Ground next to Mount Ida. In 1974 the Troy Record newspaper complained about the deterioration of the cemetery which lies on the northern level of the park near the Poestenkill.**

Heartt was very active in local affairs and community minded. In 1832 he was a delegate in the state convention of the Young Men's State Convention. He was nominated in the 8th ward for alderman in 1837 and was elected Alderman in 1837-38 and 1838-39 and was a very active alderman serving on a number of standing committees: Navigation, Waterworks, Lamp, Auditing, Expenses of the Fire Department, Market, Street Inspector/highways, the Committee to Settle the Account of City Collections the Account of the Overseer of the Poor. He was put on a committee to confer with the trustees of the Troy Academy to authorize the union of that academy with the Rensselaer Institute, which became Rensselaer Polytechnic Institute. He also was on a committee to change the building of the iron fence around the park in front of the courthouse and to remove the fence crossing the park from the east line to the center of the former alley, as far south as the north line of the Female Seminary Buildings. This is the current Seminary Park, which now Russell Sage College appears to be taking care of for the city (It does not belong to the college, it is city property). It is the first village park and was donated to the city by one of the Vanderheydens earlier. In 1917 the city council formally changed the name to Sage Park to honor financial donations by Mrs. Sage, but no evidence of selling it to the college exists.

In 1838 he also was involved with a small problem with the city. The council authorized themselves to make some suitable arrangements with Heartt as to maintaining the partition fence between his farm on Ida Hill and the city's Mt. Ida Burial ground that was located down the hill and north of his property.

The following year, in May, Albert left the firm of Jonas C. Heartt and Brothers – with his brothers Jonas Coe and Philip T. He was also spending time in his gardens and orchards on Mt. Ida, and like many of the upper-class of the time, competing in the local county fairs and agricultural organizations for prizes on who grew the best apples, pears, flowers, etc.

He was not reelected to the city council in 1839. He lost to Moses I. Winne. And even though he withdrew from J. C. Heartt & Brothers in 1841, he and his brothers had legal problems when they failed to apply a payment from a customer to his debt. They were sued and lost the case. Heartt went on to tend to his gardens and continually won premiums in the events put on by the NYS Agricultural Society, NY State Fair, Albany and Rensselaer Horticultural Society, and others, winning for his peaches, pears and plums, roses, dahlias, along with homemade silk from his raised silk cocoons.

In 1842 he put an ad in the paper to sell some of his garden material:

"For Sale, 100 Isabella Grape Vines, 1 to 3 years old; 100 Cherry trees; also, a splendid variety of garden Roses and other shrubbery, 150 variety of new double dahlias; also peonies, lilies, delphiniums, and other varieties of flowering plants and shrubs; 10,000 of the best kinds of hardy mulberries. AP Heartt."

This same year he put up for sale his Washington Park House and several building lots:

"For sale, or to rent. The subscriber offers for sale his former residence, corner of second and Washington streets, with or without the ground attached. If sold, two-thirds of the purchase money can remain upon bond and mortgage.

Also, twenty five eligible building lots, in the lower part of the city, between Liberty and Adams Streets on a credit of from 5 to 20 years. AP Heart."

Over the years several landslides took place on Mt. Ida from undermining the hill from excavating at its base (see the column on Troy avalanches at http://blog.timesunion.com/rittner/you-better-run-for-you-life/3238/). Heartt was blamed for the one in 1843 and it appears that one of the local newspapers and others were putting the blame unfairly on him. He wrote a defense on Feb 23, 1843 in the local Troy paper. Here is what the newspaper said first:

"The Slide. A communication from Mr. A.P. Heartt, on the subject of the late slide, will be found in this morning's paper. It will be seen that his views as to the cause of the slide differ from those expressed in this paper on yesterday. The public will thus have both sides of the question, and will be enabled to form their own conclusion as to which is the correct side. Mr. Heartt's explanation of the cause of the slide, is certainly very plausible. On the other hand, we have the testimony of several credible witnesses that the earth on the level at the base of the hill was greatly agitated and thrown up like the waves of the sea."

Heartt's defense published that same day was somewhat to the point:
"For the Testimony

I was much surprised on reading in this mornings Whig the cause given of the last avalanche from Mount Ida. They must have originated from persons implicated in undermining at the base of the hill. The recital of events passed, are, I believe entirely erroneous. Being the owner of the land, and having observed the operation of different chores transpiring almost daily since the ground was broken in 1829 to get earth for filling up the low grounds. I think I could give to any geologist, understanding the formation of the hill, a satisfactory explanation of the avalanche.

As to the comparative quantity of earth, now lying at the base, and hole left in the hill, any person must go on the summit, near the edge of the precipice, to enable them to judge with any correctness, and they must have been acquainted with the situation of the ground before the avalanche to enable them to estimate the proportion, now prominent, belonging to the old, which was never removed, and the last avalanche.

The gentleman (I suppose, from what I have heard one of the contractors), must have been terribly frightened to have seen and heard what he did, though he must have been expecting a fall of earth, as I had continually, for the last eight months or more, been warning them of the effects of their undermining at the place they have been digging, and threatening them with prosecution for destroying the value of my property by their wanton removal of sand and gravel while there was an abundance of clay remaining of the old avalanche. Little did I think that in falling it would have been thrown so far forward as to have endangered any dwelling.

As to the stream of water, it broke out in 1836, tapping a fine well and spring near it which had been in use nearly 20 years, although it varied in quantity until about May 1837; it has varied but a trifle at any time since, not even in the dry season of 1841; it has never ceased to flow for a moment, and now, since the last slide, this quantity appears to have increased a trifle, and very likely in a short time will be the same never varying rivulet or spring it has been for the last five years.

The base of the hill, with the front, presented for the last year or two at the surface and 20 to 30 feet below and above, is made up of strata of sand and gravel, above which is a stratum of clay, mostly blue, varying from 20 to 40 feet; above which is a body of sandy and gravel varying from 10 to 30 feet deep. The front now presented is yellow clay rising to within 30 feet of the summit, surmounted with gravel and sand. Between the body that has moved down and the hill remaining, there appears a body of sand and gravel to have laid or stood nearly perpendicular 60 to 80 feet, and of course diverging, in a great measure, the clay that moved from that remaining. Their undermining has caused a settling of the whole mass and made perceptible cracks or fissures in the clay. Of course the great body of clay has absorbed a large quantity of water from the superincumbent earth which would otherwise have found vent, over or under its own body, through the sand or gravel. The surface of the hill being frozen has no doubt helped to accumulate power by preventing a tipping over of the mass, at least of the surface, of 20 to 30 feet of gravel; the weight of which added to that of the clay filled with water and hanging or laying some 30 feet above the front base has all tended, combined with the wet slippery state of the blue clay, to throw out with great force the blue clay, which with its own weight and the descent it most necessarily make, acquired an impetus that carried or slid it over some 3 to 500 feet of nearly level ground, and causing the destruction you have described – the gravel, sand,

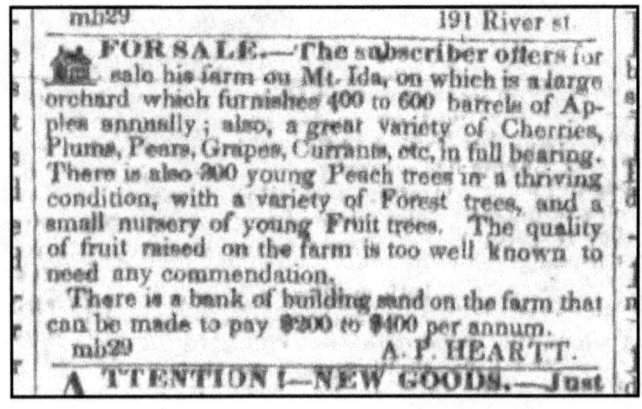

and detached quantities of clay following after with much less rapidity. I could compare the shooting out of the blue clay to pressing a fresh cherry stone between the thumb and finger until forced out by the pressure.

My only object is giving you the above facts and my own conclusions, has been to give as correct an explanation of the causes which led to the unfortunate catastrophe as I think can be given, and to let the public know that if blame is to be attached to any one it should not be to me. As to the loss of property mine has been far greater than other persons. A.P. Heartt."

Of course it didn't help that the night before this paper was printed there was another avalanche about 6 o'clock in the evening a few feet south of the one that occurred the previous Friday and subject of the above Heartt defense. It carried off the woodshed of a house belonging to Henry Clark. The house escaped damage. One observer said that the clay was *"in a state of liquefaction almost, and ran over the level ground with considerable rapidity."*

In other words, if you keep digging out dirt from the bottom side of the hill, there is a good chance that the dirt above that hole you left is going to cave in. If you look at the northern most wall of Mt. Ida, you can still see the scars of one the avalanches.

During 1834-35, 1840-41, 1843 and 1862, Alexander Dallas Bache from the Smithsonian conducted a magnetic survey of Pennsylvania and surrounding states determining a number of places to record iso-magnetic lines, dip, and intensity. During his 1843 survey he took a reading from one of the orchards of Heartt and his observations were recorded as *"in orchard of Mr. Albert P. Heart, under apple tree, third from yard fence, 65 paces S.W. From house; above river 230 feet."*

He also took a reading under a large poplar tree in a Dr. Potter's garden 15 yards from the SW end of Union College in Schenectady.

In October of 1843, perhaps as a peace offering to the Troy Daily Whig for their avalanche story back in February, Heartt sent the editors of the paper some of his famous peaches. They wrote:

"Large peaches. Mr. A.P. Heart has sent us some fine peaches from his garden in this city; the largest of which measure 10 ¼ inches in circumference, and weighed 9 ounces. This is the largest peach we have seen this season. If any of our friends can produce a larger one, we shall be very happy to eat it."

The year 1844 was the last for Heartt on Mt. Ida. In March he advertised both his farm on Ida Hill and townhouse in Washington Park were for sale:

"For Sale – the subscriber offers for sale his farm on Mt. Ida, on which is a large orchard which furnishes 400 to 600 barrels of apples annually; also a great variety of Cherries, Plums, Pears, Grapes, Currants etc., in full bearing. There is also 300 young peach trees in a thriving condition, with a variety of forest trees, and a small nursery of young fruit trees. The quality of fruit raised on the farm is too well known to need any commendation.

There is a bank of building sand on the farm that can be made to pay $200 to $400 per annum. A.P. Heartt."

The second ad:

"For sale or to let, the subscriber offers his former residence on Second Street, fronting Washington Park, for sale or to let, either with or without the garden attached. It is considered the most desirable residence in the city, the garden furnishing a large quantity of fruit, and well filled with shrubbery and flowers. Also a number of vacant lots on First, Second, Third, Fourth, Fifth, and Hill Streets. A.P. Heartt"

Along with his advertisements of offering to sell his homes, he also offered his annual offerings of trees, flowers and flowers:

"Grape Vines and Fruit Trees – 100 Isabella and Catawba grape vines, 2 to 4 years old; a few hundred of those fine varieties of peach, cherry, pear and plum trees, raised on Mt Ida, and so well known in this vicinity. A few large Lindens, Ailanthus, locust, maple and hardy Mulberries for shade trees;

10,000 hardy mulberries for feeding silk worms, at 5 cents each; Also a variety of fine roses, peonies, and garden shrubbery, Mt. Ida April 11, 1844 A.P. Heartt"

In May, Henry Vail purchased the Heartt Mt. Ida farm, all 44 acres of it, for $12,500. Heartt then lived the remaining years of his life at 50 Second Street.

Five years later in 1849, A.P. Heartt died.

The Henry Vail Years

Henry Vail purchased the Heartt estate in 1844 a month of so after it was up for sale. Henry Vail was another early settler of Troy.

In 1805 Vail went into partnership with Laban Gardner forming Gardner & Vail and took part of the store occupied by T. & I. McCoun offering *"for sale, at reduced prices, an extensive assortment of dry goods and groceries."*

In 1807, Henry and his brother George went into dry goods under the name H. & G. Vail and in 1815 changed to wholesale dry goods. In 1830 they took in Ebenezer Proudfit but Henry retired two years later with a fortune.

In 1811 he married Eliza Selden, daughter of Charles Selden, Esq. Three years later in 1814 he was a director of the Farmer's Bank in which his father-in-law was one of the first directors. Also in 1814 he and others applied for a charter to form the Rensselaer and Saratoga Insurance Company which lasted 26 years before it was replaced by the Troy Insurance Company in 1831.

Vail was interested in politics. In 1832 he was a delegate for the Democratic State Convention supporting Van Buren and Jackson. In 1834 he was the Third Ward Democratic Supervisor-elect and in 1835 ran for Congress. Not everyone was happy about that.

The Daily Whig editorial on October 31, 1836 reported:

"Electors of Rensselaer County, look out for the Congressman whom you will send to represent your interests in the national legislature of some years to come. Shall he be Hiram P. Hunt or Henry Vail? Shall he be a man who is friendly to a judicious tariff, friendly to the existing compromise of the tariff question – a man who from regard to the prosperity of his constituents, will not consent to any alteration or modification of it – who knows his Congressional District to be an agricultural and manufacturing District, and deeply concerned in a question of this kind? Then vote for Hiram P. Hunt, a man who will stand by your interests on this subject, and on all others, to the last moment. Will you elect for your congressman a man who is brought forward by the leaders of a party, who would at once sacrifice the tariff to promote their views and ambition – who to gain the favor of the South and to sustain Martin Van Buren, should he be elected President, would at once yield the tariff, if it become necessary – would disregard national interests to subserve private ambition – would make our country depended upon foreign nations – if you wish such a congressman then vote for Henry Vail; and further if you wish, when your interests, honor, and prosperity as a Congressional Distinct, are assailed, a man on the seats in Congress not on the floor, who will be a mere cipher there - who cannot open his mouth upon any question that may arise – then vote for Henry Vail. We have not the least doubt that Van Buren would at any moment sacrifice the tariff, if it were in the way of his

ambition, and if he could thereby secure the favor of the southern States; and we have not the least doubt, too, that every Van Buren Congressman in this State, Henry Vail among the number, should he chance to be elected, would chime in with their master – would at once put on the collar, and follow the dictum of their leader. Farmers, mechanics and manufacturers, look to this question and its bearings, and vote according to what you know to by your own interest and the interest of your Congressional District."

They didn't let up either. The Troy Daily Whig on November 1, 1836 was no less scathing when they wrote this:

"What was the Troy candidate for Congress, Henry Vail doing to aid in her distress during the last war? What claims has he had upon this Congressional District and upon his country, of a seat in Congress? What could he do should he chance to get there? Who would he get to write his speeches and then who would he get to speak them for him? We want in Congress no man who has the lockjaw all hours of the day except dinner hours."

The Albany Evening Journal on November 7, 1836 published this:

" A Van Buren United States Bank Candidate for Congress! - Henry Vail. The Federal Van Buren candidate for Congress in Rensselaer, went to Philadelphia but a few weeks since and made a personal application to Nicholas Biddle, for the establishment of an illegitimate branch of the "monster" at Troy! Had the Whig party nominated such a man, the stones in the streets would have been thrown at them. But the Albany Argus, with all its canting, hypocritical horror of the United States Bank, supports a man for Congress who has recently applied for one of its branches at Troy!

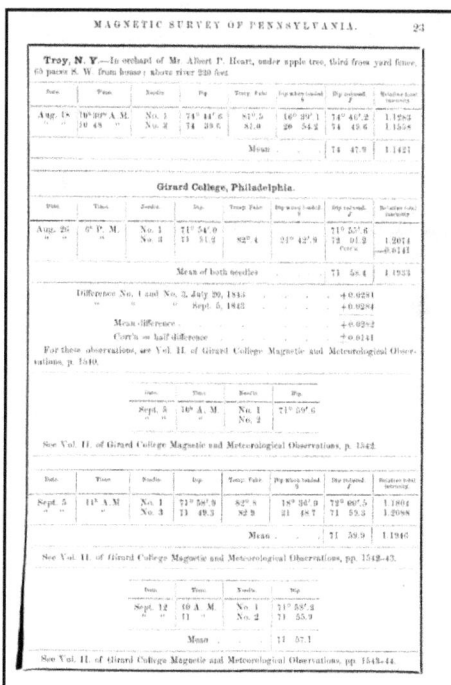

Another newspaper on the same day published this:

"And why not? Mr. Van Buren, and Gov. Marcy, and attorney general Butler, have all applied to Mr. Biddle, in writing, which we have seen, for a branch in Albany! Has the Evening Journal lived so long in Albany, and yet does it look for principal, or consistency, in these Regency politicians? Mr. Vail will make a very good member of Congress. He was a thorough-going federalist, and has only drawn a very thin veil over his principles for the occupation!"

With all that thrown at him, he was still elected as a Democrat to the 25th Congress (1837-39). During that tenure he became one of the directors of the Merchants and Mechanics Bank in Troy. He was renominated for Congress in 1838.

One local paper wrote this:

"Ancient Federal Maxims"

Electors of Rensselaer! Can you vote for HENRY Vail for Congress, after reading the Federal Maxims in the Argus, and calling to mind that this Henry Vail, now Sub Treasury Member of and Candidate for Congress was throughout one of the bittered and most intolerant FEDERALIST!"

He lost reelection as many Democrats did in what was called the Tornado years in which the Whigs won almost everything. He returned to Troy and in 1844 purchased the elegant summer residence of A.P. Heartt, Esq. on Mount Ida. He spent the next few years in business dealings. In 1846 he was elected as a director of the Rensselaer and Saratoga Railroad, but also spent a great deal of time in his gardens and orchards on Mount Ida raising crops and submitting his results at the local fairs and agricultural events. He often won for his apples, grapes, flower arrangements, celery, blood beets, and four varieties of eggplants.

This is Philip Heartt's mansion, later A.P. Heartt, then purchased by Henry Vail. Known as the Casino at Prospect Park until it burned.

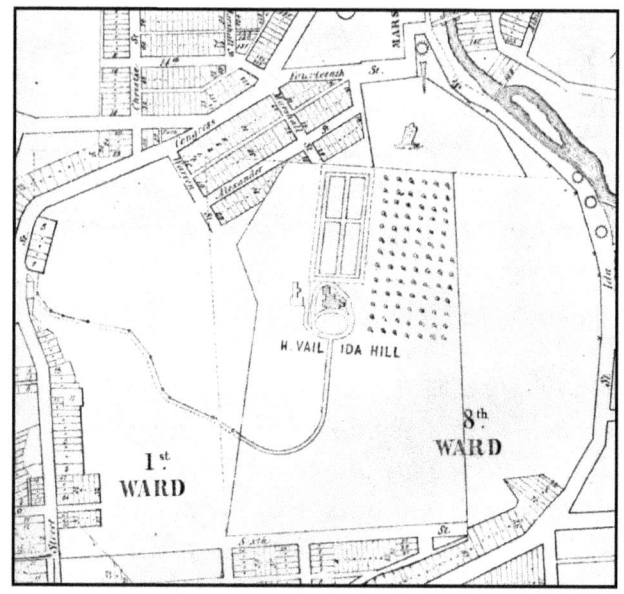

1845 Map showing Mt. Ida with only Henry Vail (old Heartt Mansion) living here. West is at top of map.

It appears that he spent most of his latter years at Mt. Ida tending to his gardens and orchards and winning many prizes at the local Ag fairs and events. His nephew David and brother George also contributed. What one will notice is how many varieties there were of apples, pears, plums, and other fruits. Now, when one goes to the local supermarket be aware of how few choices there are.

Vail died on June 25, 1853 at Mt. Ida of throat cancer. The Troy Daily Times published this two days later:

"Death of Henry Vail

The Hon. Henry Vail died on Saturday afternoon, at his residence on Ida Hill. His disease was a cancerous affliction of the throat; and his age was 70 years. The funeral takes place this afternoon at 4 o'clock at St Paul's Church.

Mr. Vail was one of the pioneers of our city, having resided in it from early youth; a prompt sagacious, honorable and highly successful merchant, and one of our most enterprising, liberal and useful citizens. He enjoyed to an unusual degree the respect and confidence of his fellow citizens, who on one occasion elected him to Congress. He was a worthy compeer of such men as George Tibbits, Stephen Warren, John Paine, and others, who left upon the city an indelible impress of their integrity and indomitable perseverance.

Mr. Vail entered the mercantile business with his brother George Vail about the year 1810, and continued in it until he amassed an ample fortune. He was married in 1813 to Miss Eliza Selden (A sister of Dr. Selden, late of this city) by whom he had a female child which died in infancy in October 1814. Mrs. Vail died on the 5th of February 1815. Mr. Vail did not marry a second time, and left no children.

In politics, Mr. Vail was a democrat, and in 1836 was nominated and elected to Congress by the democratic party of the county. His competitor was the Hon Hiram P. Hunt, over whom he had a majority of 208 votes. Mr. Vail's public services ran through the first half of Mr. Van Buren's Administration, which he cordially supported, against the apostasy of Tallmadge, Foster and Degraff, of the New York delegation. He never undertook to take any part in the discussions, but his influence with committees and individual members was felt and acknowledged. In 1838 he was nominated with the greatest unanimity for reelection, but defeated in the canvass. This was one of the "tornado" years, in which the Whigs swept the board of almost everything democratic. The State and county both went largely Whig. Mr. V's former competitor, Judge Hunt, received a majority of between 400 and 500. From that year he had not at any time actively engaged in politics, although he continued to give democratic men and principles a steady support. Shortly after the death of Albert P. Heartt, Esq. he purchased the beautiful suburban residence previous occupied by that gentleman, where he resided until his death, principally engaged in the management of his large property. His spare time was divided between a large and well chosen library and horticultural pursuits.

It is supposed Mr. Vail has left property to the value of half a million dollars, in bonds and mortgages, stocks, government securities, &c -. We believe that he possessed but little real estate excepting the beautiful place on which he resided during the last years of his life, and where he died. We do not know what disposition he had made of this large estate, but we presume it is not doubted that the bulk of it will go to a nephew, the surviving son of his brother George."

It does appear that Henry's nephew David Thomas Vail was the recipient of at least the mansion on Ida Hill since the city directory of 1854 lists him living on Ida Hill. The 1858 Barton map of Troy clearly labels the Vail House now as Riverview and the D.T. Vail residence. The 1858 map also shows a new mansion north of the Vail house, the cottage designed and built for Nathan B. Warren.

David Thomas Vail, the Nephew

David Thomas Vail was a man of his own history making. A graduate of Williams College, he married Phoebe Bloom Hart, an Emma Willard Graduate (Troy Female Seminary) on November 20, 1838; she was nineteen.

We know that D. Thomas Vail, as he was known, went into his father's business and became a director of the Merchants and Mechanics' Bank of Troy becoming president in 1850. He was also vice president of Troy Union Railroad Company and escorted Abraham Lincoln on the train when he stopped and campaigned in 1861.

He also continued the agricultural pursuits of his Uncle Henry and won several awards in the various Agricultural fairs and events around the Capital District. It appears that his specialties were handmade bouquets, green houseplants, and centerpieces.

David moved into the Mt. Ida mansion in 1853 when Uncle Henry died and is listed in the city directory there in 1854. After that the Vail Mansion is known as Riverview and appears with that name on city maps. The disposition of his house at 2 Park Place is unknown but he may have sold it.

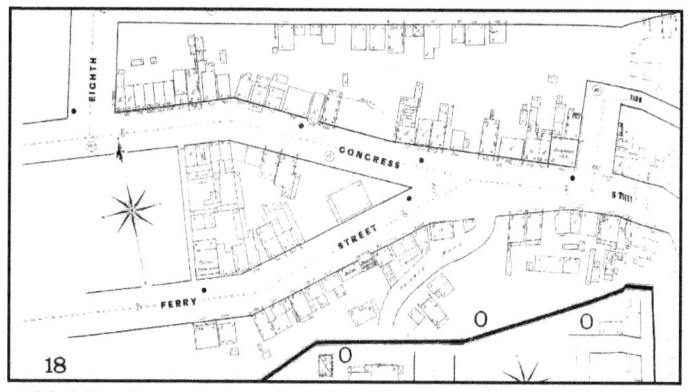
1885 Sanborn Atlas showing original Vail or Cottage Road just past Ferry Street.

Unfortunately his reputation tarnished in 1878 when he was found to have embezzled thousands from the bank to fund a failing mill in Schaghticoke that he served as president. His son-in-law and brother-in-law were also implicated. In ill health, he died on February 5, 1882. His daughter found him dead in his bedroom at Mt. Ida. It was shortly after that when the Vail Mansion was purchased by the Warren family.

The Warren Years

Nathan Bouton Warren seems to be the last person along with his brothers to purchase a part of Mount Ida for private use. Born in Troy, to wealthy parents, Nathan B. Warren was an author who had an honorary doctorate of music from Trinity College, which his family helped finance, and was a well respected businessman in Troy. His wife Mary Bouton helped establish the Mary Warren Free Institute, started by Nathan's mother.

Illness when he was young inhibited his attendance at a classical school so he sought refuge in music and reading. He and his friend Irving Paris, a nephew of Washington Irving, became lovers of books. He was interested in church music, at the urging of his father, but he became blind at age 10 by an accident, but it did not stop him from composing. In 1840, he regained part of his sight through an operation but it did not continue and became permanently blind shortly after.

He had a brother George Henry Warren, born in 1823, who made his living in New York City after graduating from Union College in Schenectady and became a prominent lawyer and financier. He also married Mary Caroline Phoenix, granddaughter of Stephen Whitney, the famous merchant of the time. His brother Stephen Eliakim Warren spent most of his time taking care of the huge Warren Estate here in Troy. His sister Harriet was killed in a freak accident being thrown out of a sleigh in 1859. She was married to Maj-General Edmund Schriver, an officer in the Civil War.

Nathan inherited a large estate from his father and continued to purchase large amounts of real estate, and build homes. He was a director of the Troy and Greenbush Railroad and the Whitehall and Northern Railroad.

The Warren family had built the Church of the Holy Cross on 8th Street and the Warren Free Institute, which he and his wife contributed to financially, along with brothers George and

Stephen. Architects involved in the church and school were Alexander Jackson Davis, Richard Upjohn, and Henry Dudley. After a visit in 1841 to England he came back and introduced choral service in 1844 to his free church and is reported to have been the first in the country. He was a trustee in General Theological Seminary in New York City and a vestryman in St Paul's Church and along with being a trustee of the Warren Free Institute for Poor Girls founded in 1846. The Church of the Holy Cross was one of the first free Episcopal churches in America. The Free School continued to grow from some 17 girls in 1835 to having to move across the street to the old Vanderheyden Mansion in 1844. That building burned in the Great Troy 1862 fire but not before some 700 girls went through the free school system. The building that is there presently on 8th Street was built in 1863.

Nathan composed several anthems and several books on musical topics. He received his honorary Doctor of Music from Trinity College in 1837 as recognition for his services (read that major financial contributions). He wrote two operettas, musical anthems, and some books. He never married.

In December of 1868 his Christmas book was reviewed in the local press. It was glowing--The Albany Argus wrote in December 19: *"An Attractive Christmas Book – Messrs.' Hurd & Houghton publish today a book by Mr. Nathan B. Warren, of Troy, with the title "The Holidays, Christmas, Easter and Whitsuntide; their social festivities, customs, and carols." The eye*

The original entrance to Mount Ida and Ebenezer Wilson's home and later to the Vail Mansion. Standing on Cottage or Vail's Road which began here where Ferry Street and Congress meet and at the eastern end of this brick house.

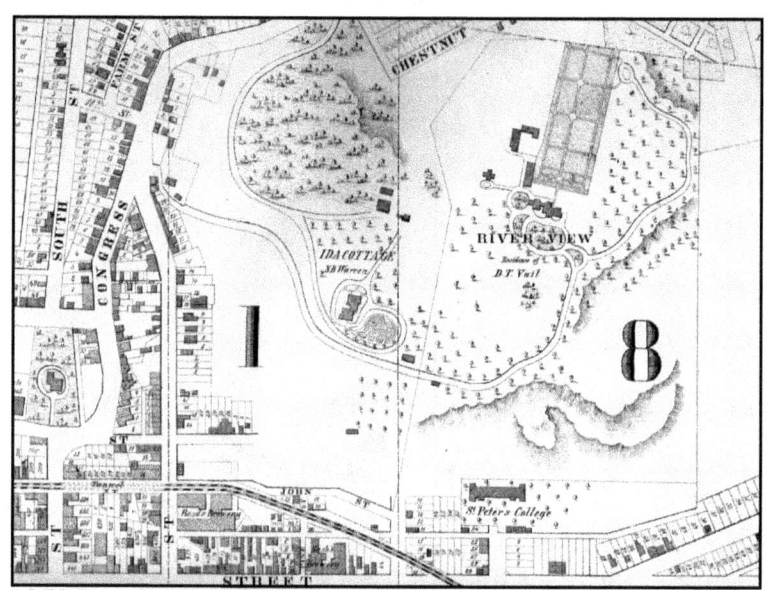
1858 Barton map showing both Nathan Warren and D. T Vail living on Mt Ida.

naturally enough is the first to be entirely satisfied with the volume. Its paper and printing are all that can be desired, and do ample credit to the well known house from which it is issued, and the illustrations by Darley are not only in his best style, but they are full of life and spirit, and admirably portray the quaint and striking scenes which the book describes.

But an examination of Mr. Warrens' part of the work more than justifies the high expectations which the mechanical part of it promises. Few men in this country are as well qualified as he for the task. His studies have long lain in this direction, and he brings to bear upon it, the loving earnestness of an enthusiast with an exquisite taste, a thoroughly cultivated mind, and a hearty sympathy with the scenes which he describes. Better, perhaps, that all, is the consecration to this sacred service of the treasures of faithfully research and careful study.

The book will deepen many hallowed associations in those who love these holy customs, and will draw many to them, who have learned already to appreciate their social attractions, and now will be led to honor them still more for their venerable antiquity and their religious sanctions.

We heartily commend the book to the large sale with it is sure to meet. And we claim our share in the local pride which attaches to its authorship."

The Troy Times also noticed it on December 19:

"A FORTHCOMING BOOK BY A TROJAN. - Hurd & Houghton will on Saturday next issue from their Riverside press an elegant and illustrated edition of a holiday work, of which our fellow citizen, Nathan B. Warren, is the author. The book is entitled "The Holidays; Christmas, Easter, and Whitsuntide – their social festivities customs and carols, which comprehensive title fully expresses its scope and contents. We have been favored with the proof sheets of the book, and a causal examination of them satisfies us that typographically and artistically no more elegant edition of a holiday work has ever been presented to the America public. The illustrations are by Darley. The author, Mr. Warren, is admirably fitted for his task by education,

taste, and social surroundings, and has given us a work which will be a source of profit and pleasure to hundreds who love to linger in the past, and who can say of the holiday customs of the olden time in the spirit of the lines so admirably quoted on the title page -

"I like them well- the curious preciseness

And all pretended piety of those

That seek to banish hence these harmless sports

Have thrust away much ancient honesty."

If you would like a copy of the book you can download it here:

https://archive.org/details/holIdayschristma00warr

Nathan B. Warren.

Known as the Cottage, Nathan B. Warren's house was designed by Alexander Jackson Davis and others. It was torn down due to lack of upkeep by the city.

His illustrator F.O.C. Darley, or Felix Octavius Carr Darley was a well-known and respected painter and illustrator who illustrated the works of writers such as James Fenimore Cooper, Charles Dickens, Washington Irving, Henry Wadsworth Longfellow and more.

Nathan and his brothers were in real estate together and it appears that they may have lived in the same house. For example, in 1876 the newspaper reported that *"The Warren brothers are building a green house in the rear of their residence at Broadway and Third Streets."* Both Nathan and Stephen never married. It appears their mother lived there too. In 1869 they erected five two-story brick houses on the west side of Eighth Street, between Federal and Grand Division Streets with each building being *"twenty five feet wide, and will be finished in No. 1 style."* As late as 1885 Nathan was building two three story brick houses on the old school lot on Grand Division Street west of Eighth Street. *"The houses will be arranged for flats, three in each building. The arrangement of rooms and stairway will be entirely different from anything now in the city."* Dudley of New York was the architect and he proposed to put houses on the remainder of the lot. The houses were *"40 feet back from the street forming a fine court in front, which will be terraced down to Grand Division Street. The cost of the present improvement will be about $18,000."* In 1893 he was erecting a three-story building on Broadway for $9,000.

Not all went well with the Warren brothers. In 1870, a team of horses belonging to them broke away and ran around the main streets of Troy before finally plunging into the Hudson River at the Ferry slip (at the end of Ferry Street). One of the horses was rescued but they were out $100 from the value of the other which drowned. In 1871, Nathan lost a lawsuit against Joseph Cavenaugh, a Union soldier at the close of the war. He paid Warren *"$250 for a little house in*

1881 Panorama showing Vail and Warren Mansions.

West Troy [now Watervliet], and before a deed was given, Warren repented of his bargain, and thrust the money back in the hand of Cavenaugh. The soldier, however refused to vacate the place, claiming that he owned it, and offering the money back several times. The present suit was brought to eject him." The NY Supreme Court went against Warren. It wasn't clear why he did this since in 1873 he was selling land to others, for example, two lots in West Troy to Patrick Lynch for 320 silver dollars; a lot in West Troy to Mary Cox for 200 silver dollars; two lots to James McQuire for 400 silver dollars; to James Foley a lot for 200 silver dollars, and the following year, a lot to Thomas McKeon for $270; a lot to William Gearsley for $200, and more in the following years. By the looks of it, he may have felt he offered it too cheap since it had a house on it and only sold it for $250 when he was getting that for a lot without a house on it.

In 1880 a Dr. Ward sued Nathan and the Court of Appeals ruled against him.

"The action was brought to restrain the defendant from closing in an alley way between the premises of both parties on Fourth St. The plaintiff claimed that he and his grantors had use of the alley for over 20 years, and are by prescription entitled to continual use of it. The case was tried in 1878 before Judge Ingalls and a jury, and a verdict found in the plaintiffs favor, which was subsequently approved by the general term. The defendant appealed to the court of appeals."

The Warren Brothers were sued by the relatives killed in a landslide on Mount Ida, then called "Warren's Hill." The claim was on the grounds that the Warrens were the legal successors of Albert P. Heartt, who they purchased it from, and who had undermined the hill to fill in a meadow, and therefore responsible. The disposition of the case was not found which seems to be the result of a slide in 1891. The Troy Weekly Times reported that the suit was brought by Rev. Father Havermans, *"and growing out of the recent landslide in Havermans Avenue."* Peter Havermans was a well known Catholic priest who started hospitals, churches and schools. It stated that evidence will go back as far as the *"great landslide of 1837"* but the paper also pointed out that there were only two witnesses alive that could remember it, a J.R. Fonda of Lansingburgh and William H. Young of Troy, the famous book publisher at 9 First Street. Since A. P. Heartt was blamed for the earlier slides, it is unclear how this suit could go that far back.

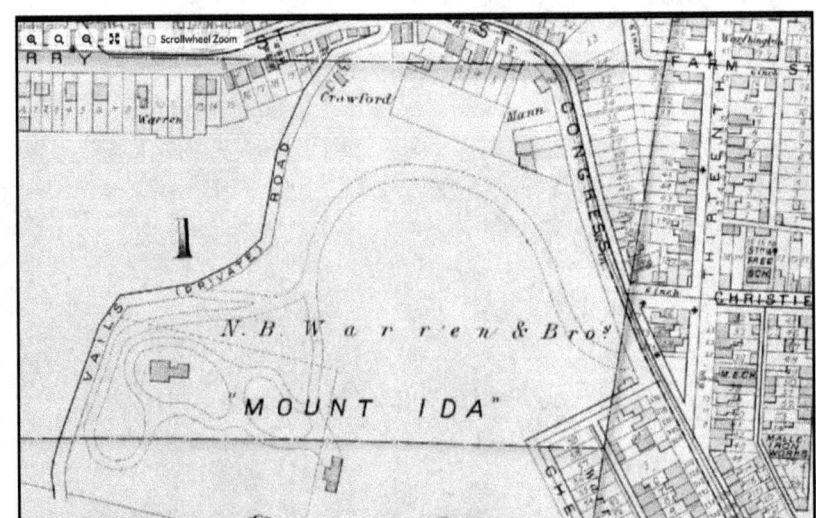

Hopkins Map of 1881 showing entire hill now owned by the Warren family.

In 1896, Anne Morrison sued him for $25,000 claiming that she was hurt when visiting his residence asking for a job. When she was leaving she was "frightened" by a small dog owned by Warren and to avoid the animal she fell by walking into an open sewer pipe and received a broken leg and other injuries that rendered her a cripple for life.

Nathan B. Warren's house on corner of Third and Broadway. Last use was as a bank.

Nathan continued his musical pursuits anyway. He was known as the "Musical Bachelor." In 1883 he wrote a holiday operetta. The paper presented it this way on December 28:

"One of the most brilliant features of holiday week was the operetta, "Hidden Treasure, or the Good St. Nicholas" given last night at the residence of the composer Dr. Nathan B. Warren. Dr. Warren, though blind, is a distinguished organist and a millionaire withal. A parlor in his old fashioned but substantial house was converted into a stage, and the operetta, giving old Christmas customs, such as bringing in the boar's head, was finely presented. Dr. Warren from early childhood has had a keen perception of colors and forms, and all dresses in the operetta were provided by him, and colors were provided with reference to scenic effect. The vocal talent was supplied largely by the choir of Holy Cross Church, of which Dr. Warren and his brothers were the chief promoters, and Dr. Tucker, the compiler of church music, rector. George Henry Warren, the NY millionaire, is brother of Dr. Warren."

Church of the Holy Cross and Mary Warren Institute.

You can download your own personal copy of

the printed version of this operetta at Google. Just type in Nathan B. Warren in the books section.

Interesting that the paper mentioned that he was blind even though he had been stricken with it earlier in life and well known at the time:

"Dr. Warren from early childhood has had a keen perception of colors and forms."

Earlier in 1871 the paper published mention of his musical abilities and wrote *"who though unable to see, yet presides at the organ of Holy Cross church every Sunday morning."*

Only five years later, the end was coming to Nathan's career when on January 13, 1888 the newspaper reported:

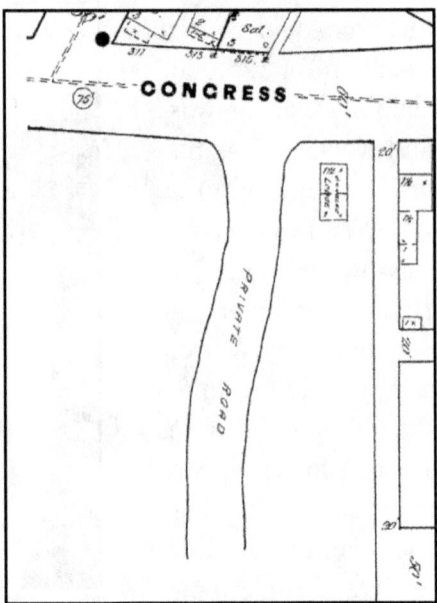

1885 closeup of upper Congress Street. Sanborn map showing location of Warren Gatehouse.

"Dr. Warren, of Troy stricken down

Dr. Nathan B. Warren, the well known organist and musical composer, of Troy, suffered a paralytic attack at his home, corner of Broadway and Third St., about 9 o'clock this morning, and his left side is useless. He was dressing when he was seized with the illness and had nearly completed his toilet. Although at an advanced age, he is perfectly conscious and it is thought that he will recover, but will never be able to play the organ again." The paper reported the next day that he *"rested well last night, and was apparently somewhat better. He was able to be dressed and sit up in a chair for a while this morning."*

Just a few days later on the 24th, Kate Sullivan, his cook at his residence, was badly burned and sent to the Marshall Infirmary and was slowly recovering. The same day, Nathan was selling off lots in the rear of Stanton's Brewery on 5th Avenue to the Union Railroad Company for $1800. While the Railroad was using them for the tracks that hugged Mount Ida and went through the tunnel to the north, they were in litigation for years. Nathan must have been sensing the end coming and wanted to get his things in order.

However, he seemed to have recovered from his condition.

In 1890, *"Prof. William Dressler of New York whose name is well known in musical circles, was visiting Dr. Nathan B. Warren at Mount Ida"* and may have been in attendance when Nathan presented another one of his operettas. The paper described it:

"The Christmas operetta composed by Dr. Nathan B Warren and entitled "Santa Claus: or, the Holly and the Mistletoe: will be given Monday afternoon, December 29, at 5 O'clock PM at Dr. Warren's residence on Third Street. The music of the operetta consists of a collection of carols composed by Dr. Warren during the last thirty years. There are six characters, which will be taken by Thomas Impett, Benjamin Franklin, William W Rousseau Jr., the Misses Heren and Miss Lizzie Weston."

In 1892 a portion of the Warren residence, built in 1826, was torn down on Third and Broadway to make room for two new stores to be built there. His house was going to be remodeled for use in business and he moved to his Mount Ida cottage for the rest of his life. In 1893 his residence on Third and Broadway was taken over by The Pafraets Dael Club, composed mostly of prominent young businessmen of the city. Originally it was going to be called The Mohawk Club but Schenectady beat them to it. The building was a bank in recent times.

The year 1892 was not a good year for Nathan. Brother Stephen died on February 7, 1892. He spent most of his time managing the vast Warren estate and in promoting the comfort of his blind brother Nathan. His other brother George Henry Warren died in April of that year at his home at 520 Fifth Avenue in New York City after an illness which originated in an attack of paralysis five years previous. He was 69. When Stephen died his will was found and was written 45 years previous to his death without any changes made. His brothers Nathan, George and sister Harriet received ¼ and the rest to his mother. Unfortunately, since George died a few months later, his sister was killed earlier in 1859, and mother was dead in 1859, most of it probably went to Nathan.

To make matters worse, on November 27th, 1896, now probably living alone, his Mount Ida home was broken into and a bronze clock, valued highly as a relic, and a buffalo robe were stolen. It does not say if he was home then. However, around four in the morning police officer Costello arrested the "notorious Jack Fay" after finding him with the clock in his possession. He was indicted and arraigned for burglary in the second degree but Fay pleaded not guilty to burglary. He agreed though to plead guilty to Grand Larceny.

Nathan died in 1898. During that year, the largest appraisals of land ever in Troy was placed on the estate of Nathan. The amount of income tax levied was $19,000. He also left $240,000 to the Episcopal church of the Holy Cross. The following year a bill was introduced into the Assembly that allowed the Mary Warren Institute to increase the numbers of trustees to nine, giving it authority to hold property bequested by Mary Warren and Nathan B. Warren. Ironically the bill introduced by Assemblyman Hutton in the increase of trustees to the institute stated that one condition was that no more than three trustees can be women. Ironic since this was a free institute to help poor girls and women. Trinity College was given $10,000 for the Hobart professorship. His estate was finally settled on December 13, 1900 with $120,000 going to the Mary Warren Free Institute. He left money to establish the "Stephen E. Warren Foundation Fund" in honor of his brother to the Institute and there were five prizes ranging from $50 for

Mt. Ida with Warren mansion tower visible. Left photo was taken c. 1900 from Troy Seminary Steeple; right photo c 1900.

first to $25 for fifth to girls at the school who exhibit *"excellence in character, deportment and scholarship."*

Before he died in 1898, he was earlier interviewed in the July 1898 edition of Werner's Magazine about Lawn Plays and festivals, written by Livingston Russell. The magazine goes on to say:

"Operas for Lawn Presentation.-

Particularly novel is the production of a light opera on a lawn. I know of none more tuneful and bright, with witty dialogue, than Dr. Nathan B. Warren's midsummer holiday operetta "Cavaliers and Roundheads." It is really a historical operetta, for, as Dr. Warren explains: "It is founded on a story of the 17th century." It was written for a garden party entertainment, one of the semiannual events prepared by Dr. Warren and given on the grounds of his beautiful summer residence on Mt. Ida, Troy, N.Y. for the girls and young ladies of the Mary Warren School, which is attached to the Church of the Holy Cross of Troy. Many of the young ladies of the school and church choir (the most renowned girls' choir in this country) take part in Dr. Warren's operettas, assisted by the male singers of the choir. Dr. Warren's festivals are noted in social circles for the completeness of their presentation and scenic embellishment and illusion."

On March 31, 1902 one of Nathan's gardners died. Samuel Davidson who lived at 314 Congress worked for F.W. Farnam as a florist as well as a gardener for Warren. In 1904, another gardner/

caretaker William Fletcher Wagstaff died. He lived in a little cottage built for him close to the Church of the Holy Cross. He worked for Nathan and the Warren Estate for 56 years.

The Warren Estate heirs continued to work their real estate holdings and during 1948 and 1949 we get a good look at some of their holdings when they applied for reduced assessments on the following parcels: 1902 7th Ave (2 story brick), 133 8th (3 story brick), 728 Federal (3 story brick), vacant land on 8th valued at $3,000, 47-49 Third Street (2 story brick), 251-253 Broadway (3 story brick), 264, 266 and 268 River Streets (2 four story brick and one 2 story brick), 217-219 River Street (two 4 story brick), 61-63 Congress (two 3 story brick), 177 River (4 story brick), 188-190 Ferry Street (double 2 story brick with frame garage), 143-149 8th (five 2 story bricks).

So it appears that Nathan Warren purchased the Wilson side of Mount Ida around 1820. According to the book "Alexander Jackson Davis: American Architecture 1803-1892" by Amelia Peck (1992), Jackson designed the Nathan B. Warren House on Mt. Ida, a Gothic Revival Cottage Villa in 1838-39. It was later enlarged but not by Davis. This makes a lot of sense since Davis also designed Warren's Church of the Holy Cross. It would also make sense that the gatekeeper's house at the entrance on Congress was part of the design and included by Davis. There has been some confusion about the Ida Hill Gatehouse now located on College Avenue and owned by RPI. It has been attributed to Henry Vail but clearly it was built during the Warren building, or was it?

Davis started his own firm in 1835 and concentrated on country houses instead of public buildings and specialized in Gothic and Italianate design. Davis also collaborated with Andrew Jackson Downing who was a landscape gardener and architect. Davis illustrated Downing's Cottage Residences (1842) and The Architecture of Country Houses (1850).

According to some notes sent to me by Kathy Sheehan, Rensselaer County Historian, Warren wrote about his "Ida Cottage:"

"My health, which had been precarious for several years began to amend. I was no longer confined to the house; but allowed my natural taste for rural occupations. It had been my boyish aspiration that I might have a farm. This inclination the executors of my father's estate did not altogether oppose; but suggested that I should take land belonging to the estate on Mt. Ida and improve it. This I have done, first by making a garden on the table-land which at the time was a little better than a desert; then by erecting a cottage, in those days considered a curiosity"

This implies that either he destroyed the Wilson farm site, or perhaps it was already gone. We know that the cottage must have been built in 1838, as written, since A.J. Downing in a letter to Davis the architect wrote:

"Since I last saw you I have visited Troy to examine Mr. Warren's gem of a residence. I was highly delighted with it & think it does both you and him the greatest credit. Indeed it is quite delightful when contrasted with the "white house with green blinds' which one stumbles upon in every direction now a days."

Later in 1865, Downing writes:

"Mr. Warren's residence in Troy, N.Y. is a very pretty example of the English cottage, elegantly finished internally, as well as externally. A situation in a valley, embosomed with luxuriant trees, would have given this building a more appropriate and charming air than its present one, which, however, affords a magnificent prospect of the surrounding country."

Good thing Downing or Davis didn't live long enough to see the final outcome of the cottage but that part of the story will come later. Ironic and humorous to find Downing lamenting on what appeared to be the "vanilla boxes" of his time period popping up around the country.

Warren had added on to the cottage so that his brother George and family could live there part of the year but it appears that the architects for the addition were Richard Upjohn and Henry Dudley and not Davis. All three had worked with Warren on the Holy Cross Church on 8th Street. We know that in 1854 he added the turrets. The Troy Daily Times reported it on May 4, 1854:

"Improvements on Mount Ida.- The Warren family have erected an additional building in connection with their beautiful cottage, on Mount Ida. It adds much to the beauty of the little "villa" from the north and east. The tower looming far above the surrounding buildings gives to it an ancient appearance, and reminds one of the castles of olden time. The scenery in view from its lofty turrets must be fine indeed. We wonder that the opportunity is not more generally embraced by our wealthy citizens in occupying the building sites upon our mounts of classic name, rather than erect their costly mansions in our narrow, cramped-up streets, amid the noise and confusion of business."

We also know that brother Stephen was living on Mt. Ida beginning in 1863 and died there in February 7th, 1892. His brother George died just two months later in April in New York City. I believe Stephen may have been living in the Vail Estate during this period rather than Nathan's home since it was available and just a stone's throw from each other.
There were several Warren children born at Ida Cottage, the earliest is in 1852.

Children belonging to George H. Warren and Mary Caroline Phoenix Warren:

1. Mary Ida Warren, born on Mt. Ida July 2, 1852
2. George Henry Warren Jr., born Ida Cottage, October 17. 1855.
3. Emeline Whitney Dore Warren, born Ida Cottage, December 20, 1857.

4. Whitney Phoenix Warren, born Ida Cottage, January 19, 1860.

Children of Robert P. and Mary Ida Warren:

1. George Henry Warren Alden, born Ida Cottage, September 28, 1882.

One of the last people born in Warren Cottage was Nina Patterson, former city council member and mother of 1980s MTV video jockey Martha Quinn.

It was also Warren who put the current main park road through from Congress Street. It appears there was a road there close by already that connected to Chestnut Street called Warren Street that is now taken up by the parsonage of the old church next to it and now an RPI fraternity. Stephen Warren discussed the new road in a newspaper article on May 14, 1885, when the new road was being built:

"The Warren brothers are constructing a new drive through the grounds at Mount Ida. The drive extends from the main entrance on Congress street, north of St. Francis church, in a westerly direction to the top of Mount Ida, and then branches to the right, running around to the Warren cottage and joining the present drive that circles the hill. Another branch to the left runs to Riverview, formerly the Vail residence. The new drive is about 400 yards long and sixteen feet wide. On either side of the carriage-drive flowers and grass plats will be cultivated. To build the new road it was necessary to cut through a high bank near the hothouses. The dirt was used in filling the road from the entrance, sixteen feet high in places. The drive will be macadamized, and will render more easy access to the buildings on the grounds in case of fire. Stephen E. Warren said last evening that at the time of the last fire that destroyed one of the buildings the steamer was obliged to go all the way around the road past the "cottage" to reach the fire. He determined to build a new road. On the west and south lines of the grounds the wooden fences are being removed and replaced with barbed wire fences. "I am tired of building wooden fences for the boys to burn," said Mr. Warren. "Sunday before last we found 300 feet of the wooden fence over by the 'avalanche' on fire, and it is impossible to keep boys from stealing into the grounds. We shall extend the wire fence around Riverview also."

The Warren gatehouse is located at this entrance on the 1892 Sanborn Insurance map and labeled as "Shingled Lodge." It is also shown on an earlier 1877 Bailey & Hazen map. It was left off the 1881 Bird's Eye View map. This gatehouse has been erroneously attributed to the Vale Mansion but the timeline does not seem correct considering this road where the gatehouse stood did not exist during the Vail residency and the road to the Vail Mansion was always from the lower Congress Street side near Ferry Street. If it was indeed a gatehouse for Vail, it is possible that the gatehouse stood there originally and moved up to higher Congress location when the Warrens owned the whole mount? Probably not since we know that Alexander Jackson Davis built the Warren Mansion and the gatehouse is similar to his designs.

After the death of David Vail in 1882, the remaining estate was purchased by the Warren Brothers. It may be that Stephen lived in the Vail house to be near his blind brother Nathan, until Stephen's death in 1892. After Nathan's death in 1898, the land was controlled by the Warren heirs and it was these heirs that would become the center of attention when the city decided to create a public park. Before his death, Nathan allowed the use of the hill to witness fireworks as the Troy Daily Times wrote on July 4, 1896:

"A comfortable grand stand has been provided by John H. McGrath for those who wish to enjoy the display of fireworks on Warren hill to-night. The stand has been well connected, and there will be police protection."

So for a good century Mount Ida was in private hands but that was all about to change.

Chapter Two
The Call for a Public Park

The idea of city parks is a relatively new one. The idea was to have an open and undeveloped green space for the inhabitants of the city.

Today, Troy, including the "Burgh," has about 300 acres of parkland for the enjoyment of all its 50,000 citizens. This includes Beman, Frear, Prospect, and Seminary Parks in Troy proper, along with Knickerbocker, Powers, and the Village "Green" in Lansingburgh.

A cursory review of these parks reveal a pattern of abandonment over the last 20 years and recent rediscovery of at least one. Troy received its first park before it was even incorporated. Jacob D. Vanderheyden gave the village of Troy three lots for use as a public square on May 10, 1796. Today it comprises Seminary or Congress Park, between First and Second Streets. It was enlarged when the city traded some lots with the Presbyterian Church. Many events took place in this park throughout the years.

This early park apparently has been claimed by Russell Sage College in recent memory since they have incorporated it, with fencing and a sign calling it "Sage Park", into their massive renovation and face lift project. It does say "public common" on a small plaque at one of their entrances, but the school laid pavement in front of the old church.

The "Village Green" that Jacob A. Lansing donated to the Village of Lansingburgh on July 4, 1793, at 112th Street, now has three quarters of the park taken over by baseball fields, basketball and playgrounds and much is fenced and locked. Only about a quarter of the park is available to all residents.

In 1917, the William H. Frear family donated 22 acres of land for a park in the city's east side. Twenty more acres were donated by Jennie Vanderheyden in 1923, and another parcel by the Eddy estate culminated in the present day 150-acre Frear Park. Much if not the majority of this park has been taken over by a golf course. In fact, it's called

Troy's first park was between the First Presbyterian Church and the courthouse, now Seminary Park.

JOHN SHERRY,
THE FOUNDER OF BEMAN PARK.

the Frear Park Golf Course!

Prospect Park, also known as Warren Park sits atop Mount Ida overlooking the city, and is the subject of this book. Some have complained that most of it has been taking over by tennis courts.

The alarming trend here is that these parks were designed and acquired for all Troy citizens, the key word being "all." They have been taken over by special interest groups. Golf courses, tennis courts, and locked ball parks are not for everyone. These large special purpose areas preclude other uses. On the other hand, perhaps this is the only part of Troy's population willing to use the parks? Beman Park (1879) and Knickerbocker Park (1924) seem underutilized.

Beman Park is Troy's first real "public" park yet you rarely see anyone in it, even though it is internationally famous in paleontology circles as the place where the first Early Cambrian fossils in the world were discovered by an amateur paleontologist/Western Union telegrapher from Troy, Silas Watson Ford.

Silas Watson Ford is a name that doesn't come up often in the annals of American Geology but he made a major contribution to the field. Ford, a Troy telegrapher, was an amateur

Beman Park with its combination horse/human drinking foundation. The hilltop fountain is gone and the bronze plaques that were attached to stone monuments were stolen years ago.

Powers Park in the Burgh was given by the Powers family.

paleontologist who made some of the most important discoveries regarding Cambrian paleontology in the 19th century. He found the first early Cambrian period fossils in North America, helping to resolve a geological controversy that was going on for 30 years. In his short life span, Ford published more than 23 scientific papers. His 7-part series of geological processes in the New York Tribune in 1879 was so popular that Union College awarded him an honorary master's degree.

The Ford family was originally from Glenville, New York. Silas and his family moved to Schenectady after the death of his parents, and then to Troy. His brother, Stephen Van Rensselear Ford, went from station agent for the Rensselaer and Saratoga Railroad in 1854, to a joint partnership with George P. Ide in 1865 to make collars and cuffs. Ide & Ford located their business at 506 Fulton St.

Silas appears to have moved to Troy the following year, boarding at 208 North Second St., and was listed as a telegraph operator. His brother, Isaac, was a telegraph operator at the Union Railroad depot and probably trained his younger brother. Later, he is listed as a bookkeeper and may have worked at Stephen's collar company. The partnership desolved between Ford and Ide, and George Ide went on to become one of Troy's largest collar companies. Silas went back as a telegraph operator but his keen interest in geology finally led him to James Hall, the state geologist in Albany.

Hall and fellow geologist Ebenezer Emmons were in an intellectual battle. Emmons had proposed the Taconic System to describe the formation of the Taconic Mountains and rocks of easternmost New York and western Massachusetts. Emmons had given an older Cambrian age (540 to 505 million years ago) to these rocks while Hall said they were younger, of Ordovician age (500 to 438 million years ago). The Taconic Orogeny or mountain building period happened about 450 million years ago when a volcanic island arc collided with proto-North America (around the Connecticut Valley region). This event ran from Newfoundland to Alabama. The rocks, which had originally been deposited in a deep-water area where stacked together by these plate collisions and formed the Taconic mountain range. Originally this mountain range was as high as the Himalayas, but quickly eroded and the sediments were deposited into a shallow sea that covered most of the middle half of proto North America.

In Troy you can see this overthrust where older rocks are sitting on top of younger rocks (especially in the Mt. Ida Gorge, aka Poestenkill) and geologists attempted to explain this anomaly (now called the Emmons Thrust, earlier Logan's Fault). Ford had found fossils in parts of these rocks in Beman Park, which helped explain the older age of the rocks and in the long run helped support Emmons' theories. Eventually Emmons was proven correct (he is buried close to Hall in Albany Rural Cemetery and it's reported he is facing Hall in his grave -- poetic justice?).

Ford jumped into the fray. His discoveries of fossils of Cambrian age proved that portions of the Taconic were older than what Hall had proposed. While not formally trained in geology, early on he wrote to Hall, at the urging of William Gurley, in an attempt to get help and guidance in training in geology, his real passion. Ford had offered loans of his fossils to Hall and Hall visited Ford in Troy. In 1871, Ford published an important article in the American Journal of Science that correlated the Troy rocks to the older Cambrian period and described the first ever fossil, Hyolithes opercula, found in North America. At 23, this established Ford as a leading authority on Cambrian fauna east of the Hudson. He even had one of his fossils named after him by a leading paleontologist, in 1881. Fordilla troyensis is one of the oldest known bivalves in the world. Throughout all of this he was still a telegraph operator now working for the American Telegraph Company, then absorbed into Western Union at 249 River Street, where the City Hall was recently torn down. He was given an honorary MA in Geology in 1877 and a member of the Psi upsilon fraternity in 1875, Union University in Schenectady.

Charles Doolittle Walcott (1886) *Second contribution to the studies on the Cambrian faunas of North America*, 30 of Geological Survey bulletin issue =30 of Bulletin, Geological Survey (U.S.)., Govt. Print. Off., pp. 369.

What appeared to be a promising career however came to an early end. He temporarily worked with the US Geological Survey, got married, and was prolific in his writings. However, Ford had either an

The Warren Gatehouse, locally known as the Gingerbread House, is similar to Jackson's illustration below. Jackson built the Warren Mansion and the gatehouse was probably built at the same time.

GATE-HOUSE IN THE RUSTIC COTTAGE STYLE.

alcohol or opium addiction and always seemed to be in debt, needing to borrow money. Eventually most of the geologists he had been corresponding with or working with wrote him off. Ford had a $72.20 debt that he couldn't afford to pay off.

Separated from his wife, she tried to sell off his fossil collection of 419 specimens and 170 volume personal library to repay the debt. Ford himself had been declared legally incompetent so Mrs. Ford assumed all liability for the debt.

Her second husband sued her on the grounds that she told him that Ford was already dead.

James Hall tried to get the State Regents to buy the fossil collection but problems arose and continued to occur as they agreed to buy it then reneged on the deal. While the State bickered back and forth, Mrs. Ford died on February 24, 1895. The collection was finally purchased (no one knows who the seller was) in 1900 for $70.70 and is now in the State paleontology collections. No one knows what happened to Ford's personal library but it may have been lost in the great Capitol fire of 1911 in which almost half a million of the State's library's collections were lost.

Four months after Mrs. Ford died, Silas died at his cousins' home, William F. Hodges in Wilton, on June 25, 1895, and was buried in Schenectady's Vale Cemetery. He was 47. His death was

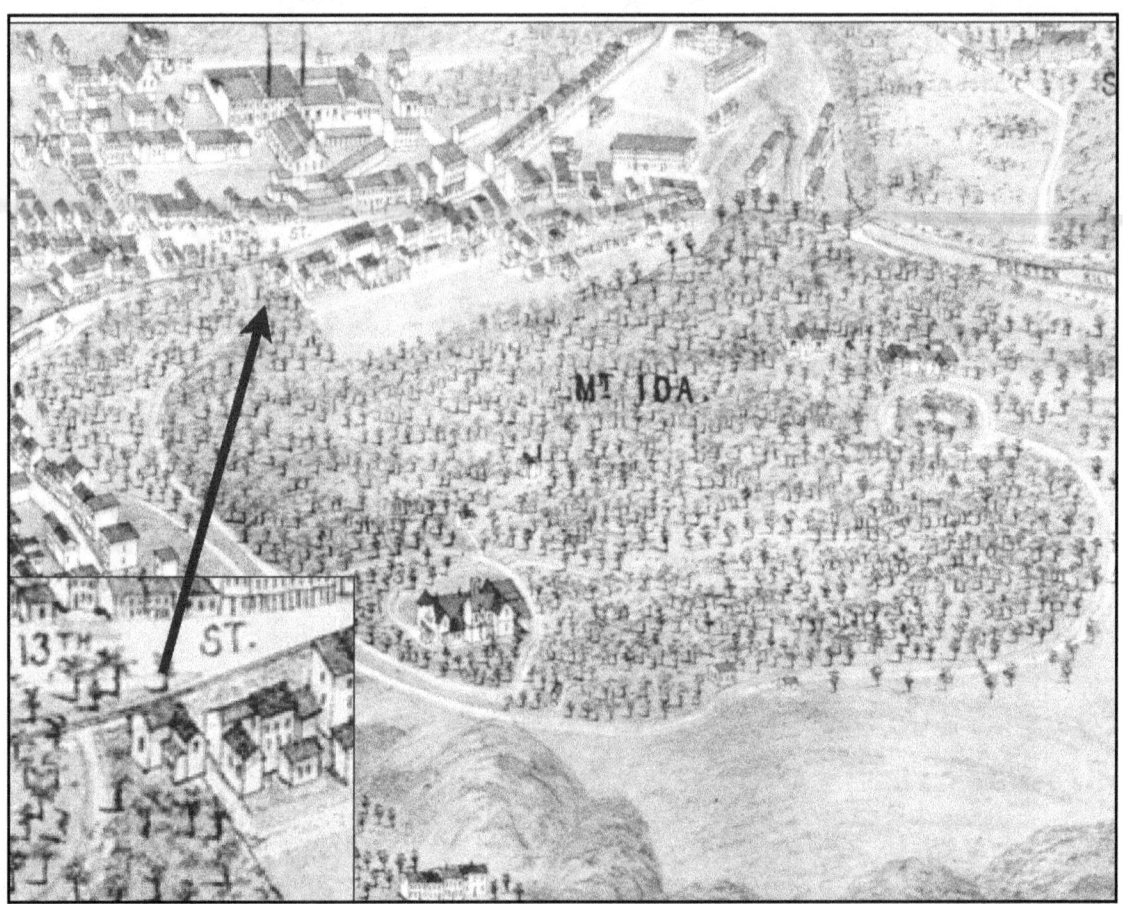

Notice on the 1877 Bailey & Hazen Map the orientation of the gatehouse. The entrance was facing the west in front of the access road. See photo of gatehouse above.

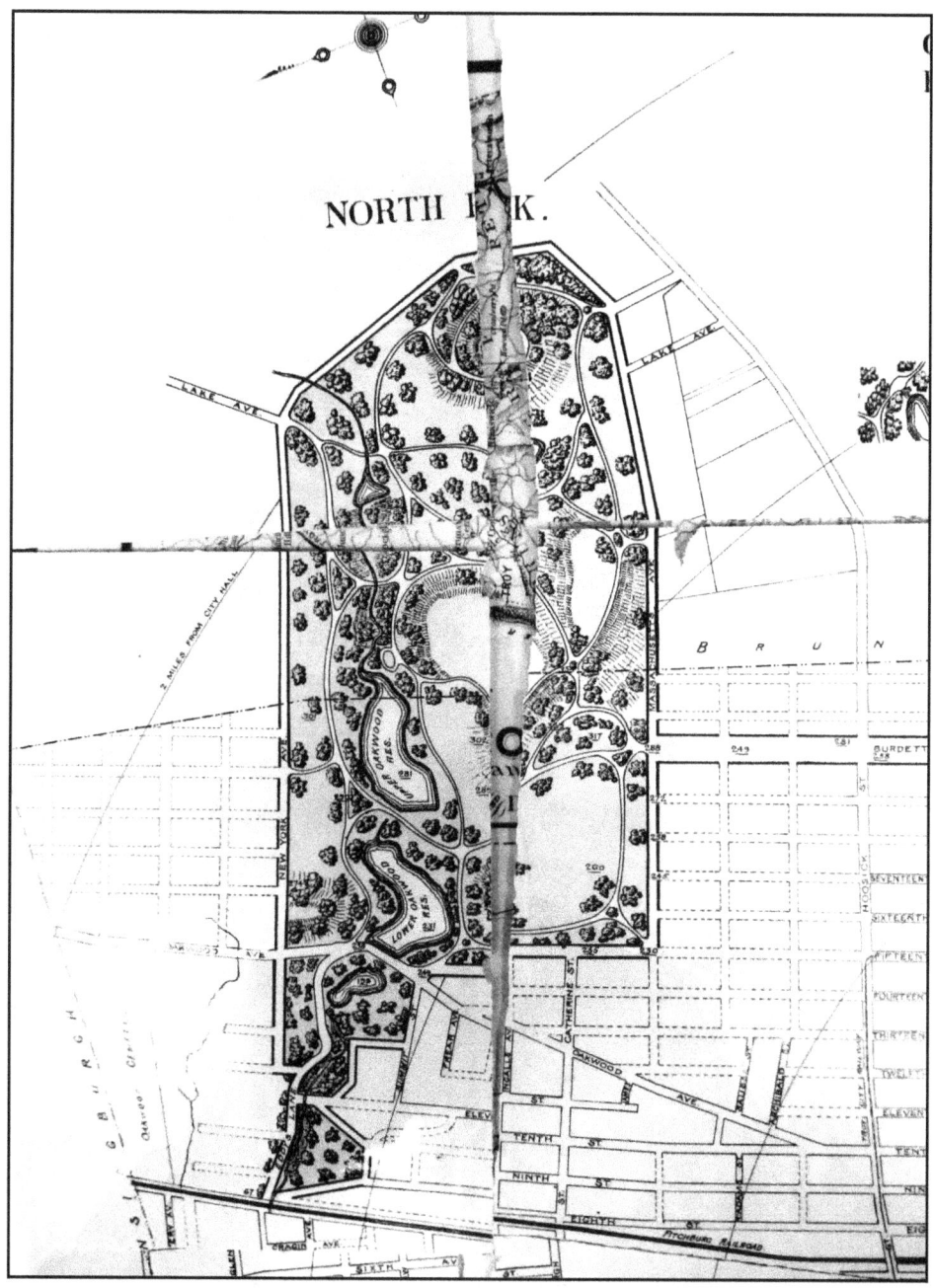

The Edgerton proposed North Park, now primarily Frear Park.

caused by "General Debility."

Regardless of his personal problems and short life, Troy's Silas Watson Ford's 20 year contributions to American Paleontology are well documented and finally given the recognition he deserved.

Perhaps the reality of the situation is that there isn't a population anymore that enjoys picnics, strolling, and passive park use. We are simply too busy zooming around in cars, talking on cell phones, logging onto the Internet, texting, or playing XBox. It's a real shame. In the meantime, playing ball might simply be better than the obvious alternative. As one developer told me years ago, *"You want green space? No problem, we'll paint it any color you want."*

The subject of city public parks came about during the late 19th century and into the early 20th century. It was called the City Beautiful Movement. It sprang up originally in cities like Chicago and Washington, D.C. and promoted not only natural beauty but also the need to create a virtuous and moral society that would lead to an increase in the quality of life. We call it today "quality of life issues" but today we include more of the social issues associated with quality of life than they did when it began when architecture was a main theme. Somehow your beautiful city full of green space and nature will sweep away all your ills and you will live in harmony and peace. Or so it was thought! Cities like Troy were gritty, sooty, crowded, noisy, violent, and very urban. Thinkers of the time felt they needed places where nature and people could interact in an urban setting as well and take the load off, relax, let their hair down. Architectural styles of the time called for order and monuments in Beaux-Arts and Neoclassical style were popular. Of course most of the promoters of this movement were middle and upper class folks worried about the large degree of urban violence and its effects on their wealth and their bodies.

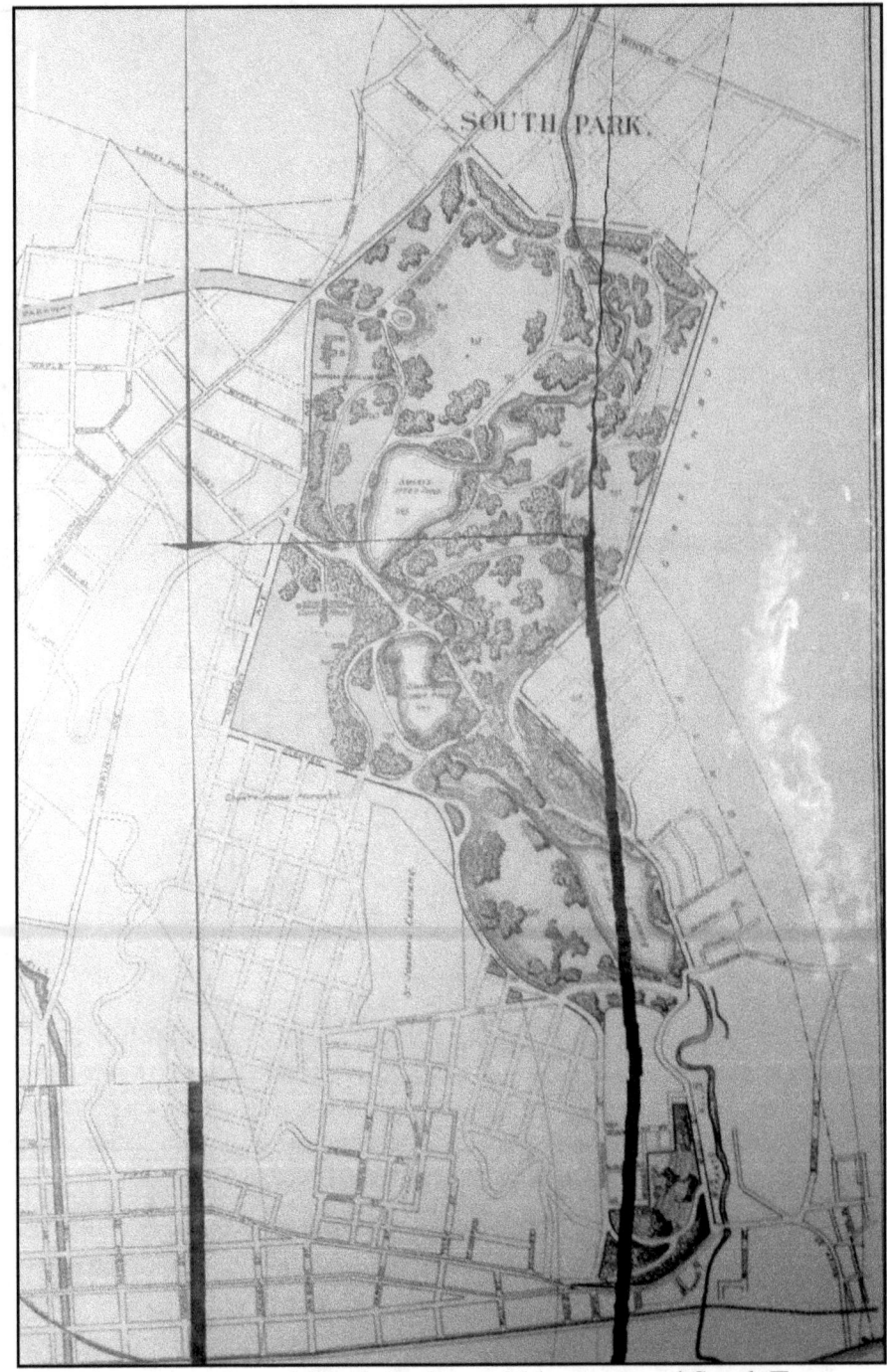

The Edgerton proposed South Park would have served South Troy residents.

So it should be no surprise that the movement swept into Troy, although a bit later than other places. It was called the Greater Troy Movement.

During the late 19th and early 20th century Greater Troy was five closely connected municipalities: Troy, Cohoes, Watervliet, Green Island and Waterford. Only the rivers separated them. They were connected by roads, bridges, rail, trolley, and ferries. With a combined population of 150,000, more than half were in Troy.

On November 10, 1890 a meeting of the newly created Citizens' Association was held. It was led by Walter P. Warren, a well known stovemaker (Troy was then the capital of stovemaking) and they took the matter of looking out for the welfare of the city in their own hands. Their major goal was the formation of public parks in the city. At the time the only real park was Beman Park, another citizen-led initiative by John Sherry in 1879. The other was a private park, Washington Park. You needed to be rich and live in any of the homes that surround it to go into Washington Park along with your "special" key when it was fenced in later. The smaller village greens such as Seminary Park and the Burgh's village park were too small for the larger population.

Proposed South Park area still has enough undeveloped land that a park could be made. Google Earth.

A resolution was read to the city council by Corporation Counsel William J. Roche:

Frear Park today encompasses much of the 1895 proposed North Park. Google map.

"Resolved, That this association favors the enactment of such legislation as will make available for the purposes of a public park, the lands belonging to the city on the east and west sides of Oakwood Avenue, known as the Waterworks property, and as well also secure lands in the southern portion of the city for similar purposes."

There was much public discussion by the association, government, and the public for a city park. The city created a Park Commission and then Mayor Dennis J. Whalen appointed George J. Brennan, Frederick P. Allen, John Squires and Henry B. Thomas to the commission. A new mayor Francis J. Molloy took over in April 1894. By February 1895 there was a report by William S. Edgerton, landscape architect with an accompanying "Map of the proposed City Parks." The legislation created under Chapter 267 of the Laws of 1892 provided for lands then known as the waterworks property east and west of Oakwood Avenue be set aside for a park. This actually became Frear Park when lands were added to the waterworks by donation from the William H. Frear family.

The addition of a park in the southern part of the city was also called for but that did not materialize. Both of these parks would have been connected via a greenway, called Burdett Avenue Parkway, now just Burdett Avenue - Beman Park would have been extended east to meet it - to Tibbits Avenue. A feeder road would have started about where Troy High School is and run northeast up crossing Brunswick Road, east of Ida Lake and Mt. Ida Cemetery, past Maple Avenue and come out near Locust Avenue crossing Pawling Avenue (then Spring Ave) where Pawling and Spring meet. Then it continued where Emma Willard School is today running across Pawling Avenue and encompassing all the land around the Wynantskill from about Ford Avenue, then running north along Clover Street, then south following the creek west down, encompassing Smart's Upper Pond (Richardson's Mill Pond), Smart's Lower Pond (Paper Mill Pond) and Burden Pond stopping at Burden Avenue. A smaller park then would have encompassed the area on the north side of the Wynantskill between Mill Street and Thompson Street starting at Erie Street.

It would have been quite the park system. However as Trojans know South Troy didn't get any respect then – as it does now. The southern park never materialized. Instead Mount Ida as a more central location was proposed instead.

Chapter Three
The Public Vs. The Chamber

Prospect Park – The Jewel of the Capital District. The Battle Begins!

As it so frequently happens in Troy there was a knockdown, dragged-out, battle between those who wanted a connected park via a speedway to go to North and South Troy – The Edgerton Plan - championed by the Troy Chamber of Commerce, its president William F. Gurley, son of one of the founders of the famous Troy surveying company, and 1200 residents who signed a petition. This was met with a group headed by John Ahern, State Assemblyman, local politicians, and 6000 residents who signed a petition that wanted to purchase Warren Hill (common name before park purchase) and turn it into a park that overlooked the city.

Both the Vail and the Warren families who had owned the hill previously had passed away and Mount Ida was now in the hands of the Warren heirs and was available.
There was a great deal of common sense in both proposals. However, Mount Ida, as I have shown, was a famous perch and visitors from around the world would stop there and get the full 25 mile panorama of the Hudson Valley. Unfortunately you needed permission to get that view as it was privately owned land. Why not allow the entire world to have access to this magnificent view - at least that was the argument presented then? The other argument was the city already owned some land in the northern part of the city. Why not connect it to some county owned land in the southern part of the city provided the county would part with it? Connect them by a speedway and the entire population would be happy?

The battle between the two interested groups was well played out in the local newspapers, particularly the Troy Daily Times. There was no nightly news, radio, cable, Internet, only the printed word and the local newspapers were keen on writing almost every detail down for their readers. Papers like the Daily Times had a morning and afternoon edition. So let's follow the battle thanks to the unsung, and uncredited, reporters of the day.

It seems the push to have a public city park in Troy came from the local assemblyman who represented the city, John F. Ahern who introduced a bill, Chapter 185 *"An Act to Provide for the Acquisitions by the City of Troy of certain lands in said city for public park purpose,"* in 1901 into the New York Legislature to create the Warren Hill Park for the city of Troy. Ahern had come to Troy in 1876 working in the trade of nickel plater and polisher, a job he was doing when elected in 1899 to the New York State Assembly as a Republican and was there until 1902 when he was defeated by Democrat John J. McCarthy. While Troy can thank him for Prospect Park, many actors of the time probably had a different point of view as he also introduced a bill to *"improve the moral quality of plays and to elevate the standard of competency among actors,"* basically creating a three member Board of Examiners where actors would have to register for $10 a year for a certificate in good standing and only holders of this permit would be allowed on any New York State stage. *"The same examiners are to judge the merits of all plays, operas, and other proposed amusements, and such as they do not like are not to be produced."* It rang of early shades of the later1920's Wil H. Hayes era, early censor of motion pictures.

It was interesting that proponents of Warren Hill were talking about the city's first public park although one would argue that Beman Park was the city's first official park created in 1878 through the efforts of Trojan John Sherry. It appears that Seminary Park (the Village Green) and the Village Green in the Burgh were not considered public parks, although they were? Most likely what they meant was the politicians couldn't put their name on them.

The introduction of Ahern's bill promoted the Troy Chamber of Commerce to spring into action. They were against the Warren Park bill based on the cost, favored the William S. Edgerton Plan discussed in Chapter Two and brought their members together on February 11, 1901:

"A public meeting of the Chamber of Commerce will be held at its rooms this evening to consider the subject of public parks in this city, and especially Assemblyman Ahern's bill providing for a public park on Warren Hill."

The Troy Daily Times recorded the results of the meeting the next day in their paper:

"At a largely attended public meeting of the Troy Chamber of Commerce last evening that organization recorded itself against Assemblyman Ahern's measure which provides for acquiring the Warren Hill property for public park purposes, and named a committee to appear in opposition to the bill before the Assembly Committee of Cities at Albany this afternoon. The committee includes President William F. Gurley and the members of the Committee on Public Improvements. The Chamber of Commerce also passed resolutions urging the acquisition of the County House Farm property and the development of a municipal park system to include this property on the south and the waterworks property on the north. A connecting boulevard is also a part of the plan, which was proposed some time ago."

Incidentally the speedway measure was brought up as an auxiliary to the park scheme. No action was taken, but enough was said to show that the proposed speedway would be an agreeable addition to the boulevard between the north and south parks.

"Opening of the Meeting

President Gurley called the meeting to order at 8:15 o'clock, saying that the session had been called by the Committee on Public Improvements to consider the question of parks in Troy and more especially the subject of the Warren Hill site, which had been selected for a public park in the measure known as the Ahern Park bill.

The Committee's Report

The report of the Committee on Public Improvements, of which John Don is Chairman, was read by Secretary Wight as follows:

William F. Gurley, Esq., President of Chamber of Commerce:

The Committee on Public Improvements of the Chamber of Commerce has met and discussed the question of public parks.

The committee begs leave to report that the former Park Commission of this city employed at large expense W.S. Edgerton, an expert park engineer, who made surveys and plans, which are now on file with the Commissioner of Public Works.

The plan referred to embrace part of the waterworks property, which is owned by the municipality; also the acquirement of the County house farm as a park for the southern section and a boulevard to extend from one park to the other. This boulevard can be extended through Eddy's Lane, which is now owned by the city, to connect with the proposed speedway in Lansingburgh. Inasmuch as the gentlemen composing the Park Commission have given this matter a great deal of care and thought, it seems wise to this committee that the Edgerton plans should be used as a basis of a park scheme for Troy – to some extent at least.

As the city charter now allows an expenditure of $15,000 per year for parks, this sum, if properly expended on property now owned by the city, will develop a system of parks second to none in the state, and at the same time will increase the taxable value of adjoining lands to such an extent as to pay the expense of the improvement.
This committee cannot see it sway clear to recommend the purchase of the Warren Hill property for park proposes for the following reasons:

First – That it would require a large expenditure of money for the purchase of the land.
Second – That the surrounding property would not be enhanced in value. Therefore there would be no increase of assessable property to the city but rather a decrease of the value now assessed on that property.

The Seminary Property

Secretary Wight also read the following:

Troy NY Feb 11, 1901
Chamber of Commerce, W.F. Gurley, President:

Dear Sir: We are taking great interest in matter of park for Troy. We send you herewith a map of St. Josephs Seminary property. Opinions differ; but it seems to us this is the ideal location for a park, being almost in the center of the city, at head of Broadway, two blocks from Union Railroad Station, with five-cent fare to South Troy. Electric cars come to same point from every direction, besides running along east boundary or Fifteenth Street. It is four blocks to Post office, six blocks from City Hall, six blocks from Hoosick Street, one block to Congress Street or proposed Nathan Warren Park. This property would be within easy walking distance from the East Side, new Brunswick district, north easterly, and to all points of city – north, east, south and west. You cannot say this of the Nathan Warren property. The view west from Nathan Warren property can only be had from extreme western part of the property, whereas from the seminary property it can be had from any part or location.

This property has also a ready made lake, where boating and possible bathing could be enjoyed in summer, and free skating in winter. The similar building would make a fine open pavilion. The people could sit on the upper floor and enjoy the nicest view in the country, and the lower floor could be used for the sale of candy, soda water, ice cream and so forth. The level part on the east makes a fine place for tennis, football, croquet and all other outdoor games. Another think in favor of the seminary property is that the vacant land surrounding it would become desirable property to build upon, and the increase of taxable property would help to pay the interest on purchase prices. We remain, very respectfully yours.

M.E. Egan & Co.

The seminary property was an early college that had a short lifespan and the site actually later became the RPI campus. RPI ripped down the "Four Towers" as it was called and this seminary building site is where the current library is located.

For the Waterworks Farm

William H. Frear sent this communication:

Troy NY Feb 11, 1902
William F. Gurley, president of chamber of Commerce, Troy, NY

Dear Sir: I would like to go on record at the meeting to-night as being heartily in favor of a public park, and believe that we cannot have it too soon but I think it very inconsistent to pay money for land and at the same time to take new land off the tax roll when we already have a charming site, which was paid for an taken off the Assessors books long ago. I mean the waterworks farm. It surely contains all the features necessary to make, at the minimum expense, a park which will compare favorable with any to be found anywhere. This land has been owned by the city over twenty years, and I have constantly wondered during that time why it has not been converted into a park years ago. It's included within its boundaries picturesque lakes, waterfalls, brooks, clumps of trees ravines, and beautiful views. Comparatively very little labor and expense would convert the waterworks property, which is already ours, into a lovely park.

*Yours respectfully,
W. H. Frear*

Frear was the owner of one of the biggest department stores in the city and it is Frear that coined the phrase: "Satisfaction guaranteed or your money cheerfully refunded." His heirs did contribute to the creation of Frear Park later.

Beginning of the discussions

President Gurley declared the subject before the meeting for discussion, noting that the committee was not opposed to public parks, but merely raised the question if the development of the waterworks property were not more feasible. The committee was unanimous in its report and President Gurley invited remarks from those present. It was noted that the matter of an appropriation of $15,000 for parks was mandatory under the White charter.

Troy Seminary was also offered as a park site. It would have been connected to Warren Hill. The old college is now the site of RPI's library. The seminary was known for years as a Troy landmark, the "Four Towers." Congress Street is in the foreground with Fifth Avenue intersecting. This was part of the original Mt. Ida, until Congress Street was cut through.

Waterworks Site Ready

William Ross was the first speaker. He asked for arguments in favor of the Ahearn measure. He knew that for years there had been a desire to open up the water works property for a park. All that was needed, he said, was to take down "no trespass" signs and put in some gates. He said the same objection would apply to the Eight Street site as the Warren Hill property – the original expense of purchase.

Paragraphs of the Ahern bill, showing that city officials were authorized to issue bonds in the sum of $160,000 for the purpose, etc. of the Warren Hill property, were read.

For a Level Park

E.K. Betts said that everybody agreed that Troy wanted a park, the principal office of which was a playground for children during summer vacations. The village of Lansingburgh had tried to promulgate such a scheme. In Albany last summer the idea had been splendidly carried out and was a success. "Such a playground," declared Mr. Betts "does more to break up the natural demoralization of a summer vacation than anything I know of. You all know my scheme, which includes Rensselaer Park, Young's Grove and the back part of that property purchased recently by Senator Murphy. There are places for two lakes, from which enough dirt may be taken to do all the grading necessary. The site is level as a walk. Children could play in it and women could wheel a carriage to it anywhere."

The Edgerton Plans

President Gurley gave a brief outline of the Edgerton plans, which embraced the waterworks property, the county farmhouse property and connecting boulevard. He reiterated the committee's position – that it was not against parks but preferred utilizing money to develop property already on hand. It was not a partisan matter, he said and it was desired that action be taken during the meeting for or against so large an appropriation as was proposed for the Warren site. He called for an expression from Mr. Don, Chairman of the Public improvement Committee. Mr. Don said his views had been expressed in the report of the committee. He favored the Edgerton plans, which he thought were remembered by all. The plans were elaborate, but interesting and especially adapted for the situation. The waterworks property was

Garnet D. Baltimore became the city's landscape engineer and designed Prospect Park. He was the first African American graduate of RPI.

owned by the city, and the fund could be immediately used in its development. He said he was not fully informed on the Ahern bill, and noted that a retaining wall would involve the expenditure of a large sum. He thought some action should be taken and the report accepted or rejected.

Three Parks Favored.

Arthur G. Sherry said in part:

We have a city of 75,000 inhabitants. So far as I know we have never expended a dollar for parks. Albany has a beautiful park of eighty acres. The Warren hill is a blemish to the city. Something must be done with it. It is an eyesore and a source of danger. The property, however, is centrally located so that a great many could reach it. I am in favor of that and the waterworks park. The city should get hold of more land, so that the value of its own property would be enhanced by a park and not somebody else's. We ought to have one large and two small parks. Many could get to the Warren site who could not to the more distant park.

A former Park commissioner

Thomas H. Campion, formerly of the Park Commission, outlined the work of the Commission in its efforts to make a park of the waterworks property. He opened by inquiring if anyone knew of a valid reason why the waterworks property, so long intended as a park site had never been developed. Mr. Campion said that during his term as Park Commissioner every effort had been made to the Water Board to comply with the law by making that territory a park. The Park Commission, however, had been unable to meet the Water Board in formal session. He said that ex Mayor Molloy had tacitly favored an appropriation of $10,000 for improving the site. The Commission had felt that it could make that site a most desirable park. The Park Commissioner had gone into their personal funds and retained counsel to compel the Water Board to turn over the property for a park, but nothing had ever come of it. Mr. Campion thought that the Edgerton plans were desirable and could easily be developed. He had no objection to the hill site, but treating the subject from a business standpoint he deemed it best to develop what the city owned without buying in more undeveloped land.
Figures on city property

President Gurley again referred to the Edgerton plans, reading from his report to the Park Commissioners. These plans called for a more extensive system than Albany's and included in its scope 200 acres of land and a fine drive.

One hundred acres available

Ex Park Commissioner Charles G. Cleminshaw declared the waterworks property afforded about 100 acres of land available for parks. The property was on both sides of Oakwood

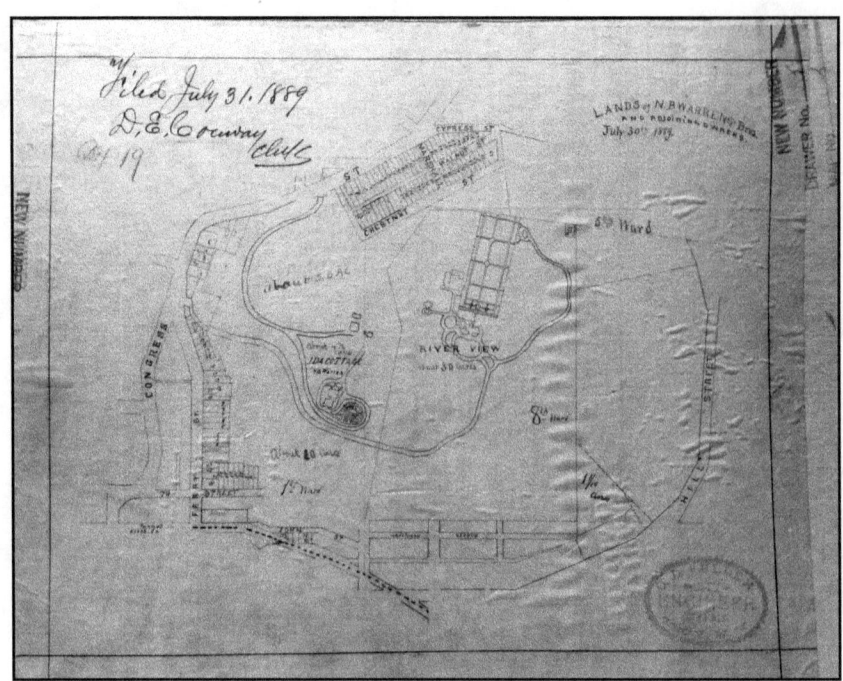

The Warren property, soon to become Prospect Park, was mapped out and filed in the city engineer's office on July 31, 1899.

Avenue, and a boulevard could be extended down Eddy's Lane to Glen Avenue and Sixth Avenue, to unite with the proposed speedway. At a small expense a fine park could be made. A lake could be made on the site in a depression which had been drained by the Waterworks Department. On the contrary, the Warren site would involve the construction of a retaining wall perhaps two thirds of the distance around it. This would be a big expense. Already there had been two landslides.

The County House Grounds

Rev. J.B. Nairn of the South Baptist Church made a strong plea for the County House Farm site and the adjoining DeFreest Farm. He advised those who had never visited the site to go at once and spend an entire day. There could be a chain of three lakes, and driveways and playgrounds for children and older people. The DeFreest Farm contained sixty acres, and could be obtained for a quarter of the expense involved in the purchase of the Warren site.

Water a Necessity

Thomas J. Phillips supported Mr. Nairn in his contention for a park in the southern section. He favored the Edgerton plans. He declared the children needed the lakes for skating and boating. If any one saw the crowds nightly on Burden Pond they would think it strange the matter had not been taken up before. There was no water on Warren Hill, he said. "A park without water would be no park at all," said Mr. Phillips. Boating, bathing, and skating would be possible in the south park, if the county farm and adjoining property were included.

An Engineers' idea

Ex Assistant city engineer Garnett D. Baltimore spoke in favor of the Warren site, saying that it was centrally located and accessible. The center of population in Troy was practically at State and seventh Streets. As a public servant the speaker had visited all sites proposed and he favored the Warren property on account of its location, its commanding view, etc. He thought the danger of a landslide could be obviated by a wall and that the property could be beautified. He was not opposed to other sites and thought nothing should be done too hastily. The idea, he said, was to get a public park for Troy.

The Cost too great.

James W. Donnelly was opposed to the Warren site. He said the Warren Hill would necessitate the purchase of a little land at a large price. It was not accessible on three sides and there was no adjoining property to be enhanced in value, and none on which buildings might be located. People would like to build along by a park or boulevard. The waterworks property offered ideal privileges, as did the proposed site in the southern section. A connecting boulevard with the speedway would make a long and beautiful drive. The beauty of the north and south park system was unquestioned, and the views from either park would be fine.

Not a cheerful view

Mr. Cleminshaw remarked that from the Warren site one had only a city view of housetops, chimneys and rear yards. If the entire park system could not be obtained at once he thought a start in the right direction would be to take the waterworks property, the boulevard and the southern site.

More opposition

J.S. Saunders said he was opposed to purchasing the Warren site. He thought a housetop as suitable for a park. He advocated starting with the waterworks property and continue until the system was well inaugurated. To obtain action of the report he moved that it be received.

Elimination and Adoption

W.H. Anderson moved that the report be adopted, and John F. Bridgeman pointed out that the reference to the speedway in the report might cause trouble later, when that measure was passed upon.

Mr. Gurley remarked that it would be wise to have some action at once, as the Ahern bill would come up for a hearing to-day in the Senate Committee on Cities.

Mr. Anderson said his object in moving to adopt the report was to place the Chamber of Commerce on record and prepare for definite action.

Mr. Campion suggested that the reference to the speedway be eliminated and the report then be adopted as amended.

Chairman Don of the committee consented to the amendment, and that part of the report was eliminated and the amended report was adopted.

To appear against the Measure

Mr. Bridgeman then moved that a committee, to include President Gurley and the members of the Committee on Public Improvements, appear before the Assembly Committee on Cities to-day and oppose the measure providing for the purchase of the Warren property. The motion was adopted unanimously.

To Wait on city officials

The following resolution was presented by Mr. Campio, and was unanimously adopted: Resolved, That the Committee on Public Improvements be and is herby directed to wait on the city authorities and urge the necessity of the city's acquiring the County House Farm property and the development of that property in conjunction with the waterworks farm into a public park system in accordance with the provisions of the White charter law.

The Committee includes President Gurley, John Don, H.S. McLeod, James W. Donnelly, Henry Galusha, John Paine, and E.W. Loth."

As a side note, E.W. Loth is the same architect who designed St. Patrick's Church that was recently torn down in Watervliet.

The Troy Daily Times continued reporting on the movement of the bill in the Assembly on February 13, 1901:

"*The Troy Park Bill*

Appearances for and against the measure- representatives of the Chamber of Commerce Attended Yesterday's Hearing in Albany – Arguments Presented – Reported Favorable – Hearing on the Dollar Gas Bill Deferred Until Tomorrow.

The Assembly Committee on Cities devoted much time yesterday afternoon to Assemblyman Ahern's measure which provides for the establishment of a public park on the Warren Hill site at an estimated expense of $160,000. There was a large contingent of Trojans at the hearing, including President William F. Gurley of the Chamber of Commerce, John Don, James W. Donnelly, Arthur M. Wight, Secretary of the Chamber of Commerce: H.S. McLeod, Francis N. Mann, Samuel Morris, Assessors Patchke and Jacobs, Alderman Beattie, James McCabe Robert T Courtney, Thomas H. Karr, William E. Smith and J.S. Saunders. The first five represented the

Chamber of Commerce and opposed the measure. J.S. Saunders also spoke in opposition. Assemblyman Ahern, Messrs.' Patchke, Jacobs, Beattie, McCabe and Smith favored the measure.

The Warren Hill Park

Assemblyman Ahern called up bill 542, a measure to establish a public park in Troy by purchasing and developing the Warren Hill site. It authorizes the expenditure of $160,000. William F. Gurley was the first speaker. He said in part:

Mr. Chairman and Gentlemen of the Committee: I with others represent the Chamber of Commerce of Troy, which sent us here to oppose the public park measure known as the Ahern bill. The Chamber of Commerce represents 400 leading citizens of Troy, and the largest taxpayers. At last night's meeting of that body instructions were given us to come here and oppose this bill. We are not opposed to public parks in Troy, but simply the expenditure of so great an amount of money as the Ahern bill provides - $160,000 – for the purchase of the Warren Hill site and its development into a park.

Park Commissions Action

In 1892 the Park Commission of Troy employed at considerable expense an expert, Mr. Edgerton, who is an engineer of the Albany Park Board, to make an examination of Troy and advise with reference to a park system. His scheme was to use the waterworks property on the north and the county farm property on the south and connect the two with a boulevard. Additional adjoining property could also be secured. The waterworks property, already owned by the city, contains more than 100 acres and is ready for improvements. Under the White charter law the Common Council is authorized to improve and extend the work of parks, and this would perhaps be sufficient to develop the system. But we do object to taking $160,000 for an inaccessible hill for a park, and we say the plan is not feasible. We say Troy ought rather to use for parks the land which it already owns, which is well laid out and admirable situated, which plan had the sanction of the Park Commission and that of an expert engineer. The southern part would be accessible to the South Troy residents and the waterworks site accessible to residents of the northern wards.

Could not be enlarged

The Warren property is a tableland some seventy five acres in extent with precipitous sides. Congress Street in on one side and the hill is really a sand or clay bank. There is no contiguous property whose value would be enhanced and there is no room for enlarging. We say instead of taking this sand heap of seventy five acres at an enormous cost take the plans approved by an engineer and make the park system of 400 acres accessible to all.

J.V. Jacobs inquired the proposed cost of the latter system and Mr. Ahern replied: "Three hundred thousand dollars."

Answering questions

Mr. Gurley displayed maps of the proposed park system, and the Assembly Committee and others examined the drawings and asked questions. These were accurately answered by Mr. Gurley. Mr. Gurley explained that the proposed boulevard would extend through Burdett Avenue and Tibbits Avenue and would build up a part of the city which needed to be developed and that the value of land would be increased. He pointed out the water advantages of the north and south parks, and closed his remarks by reiterating the position of the Chamber of Commerce as not opposed to parks, but in favor of developing its own land rather than purchasing other property.

Estimating the Cost

John Don, Chairman of the Committee on Public Improvements of the Chamber of Commerce, explained the location of Troy and Lansingburgh, now included in Greater Troy. He said the city was a long and narrow strip bounded on the west by the Hudson River and on the east by a row of hills. A small park Beman Park, was in the center of the present city. Under the plans favored by the Chamber of Commerce the waterworks property would be near the northern wards, and the County House Farm property available to residents of the southern district. It seems to the speaker that the Warrens' site was very expensive. The bill provided for an expenditure of $2,000 per acre, and, on the other hand, lands at the proposed north and south parks could, the speaker thought, be procured at an expense not greater than $200 per acre.

Speaking as a Citizen

J.S. Saunders spoke as a citizen opposed to the measure. He said that when a district sends its representative to the Assembly it expects him to lay aside self and to represent every one of the taxpayers so far as he is able.

"Where do you suppose gentlemen, this bill originated?" continued Mr. Saunders. "Did the Assemblyman consult the Mayor? Did he consult the Common council? Did he consult the Chamber of Commerce or the old Park Commission? Did he talk with the leading or the small taxpayers?"

Mr. Burnett, who was acting as Chairman in absence of Mr. Kelsey, asked if it was supposed to be the office of an Assemblyman to consult different bodies. Mr. Saunders voiced no reply, and continued. Mr. Bunrett asked: "May I ask a question, Mr. Saunders?"

"Wait till I get through," answered the speaker, and from that time on there was interruption.

Mr. Saunders continued at some length, stating that Troy needed a new hotel, a new station, the abolition of grade crossings and so many things that he hoped that the committee would protect the city of Troy from the expenditure of $160,000 for the Warren site for a park. During his remarks Mr. Saunders said he was of the opinion that the Ahern bill was originated in the office of the agents for the Warren Estate.

Mr. Ahern said that was untrue.

An Assemblyman's Reply

At the conclusion of Mr. Saunders' speech Mr. Burnett declared that he, as a member of the Assembly, as a member and Chairman of the Committee on Cities, resented the imputations and insinuations made by the speaker against Mr. Ahern. He declared that the personalities indulged in were improper and he believed without reason or foundation.

Mr. Saunders apologized for any personal remarks.

More Opposition

James W. Connelly, disclaimed any ill-feeling on the part of the Chamber of Commerce toward Mr. Ahern and declared it was merely a question of expense and feasibility that brought the opposition to the measure. As a member of the committee he had given the matter much attention, and had concluded that the Warren site was not the best and that it was expensive. His remarks concluded the opposition, and Mr. Ahern took the floor.

In Favor of the Measure

Mr. Ahern spoke for the bill, and began by stating that he had the greatest respect for the members of the Chamber of Commerce and for every taxpayer in the city of Troy, and for every resident. He made this statement to show his position. Turning to Mr. Saunders he declared: "If you have been used to dealing with crooked assemblymen, you are least dealing with a straight one now."

Mr. Saunders ejaculated: "Thank God,"

Chairman Kelsey rapped for order, and Mr. Ahern said: "I wish, Mr. Chairman, you had been here while he was speaking. He got full fling, and I would like to hand it back."

An Industrial Centre

Mr. Ahern pointed out that the bill was a measure for a public park in Troy. He had been in the Common Council and had heard all of the Edgerton plans discussed. He declared that the *opponents of his measure had failed to tell the committee that the industrial portion of the city was centered about the Warren site. The speaker declared the proposed system including the north and south parks, was all right for those who could afford the time and car fare to reach the sites, but his measure was to provide the working people of Troy a park at their door. The Warren site contained seventy five acres, and there was adjoining ground to bring the entire plat to ninety acres. The property was assessed for $134,000. The speaker quoted from the remarks of Mr. Cleminshaw and Mr. Baltimore at Monday night's meeting of the Chamber of Commerce. Mr. Ahern said he was not opposed to other parks, but he wished this one, and he thought the sentiment of the people was in favor of it.*

He quoted figures and outlined the methods of financing the matter, showing that the taxes would be very light to pay for this park and the advantages surpassingly great. He spoke of the trees on the Warrens site, the beautiful view and its easy access. He called attention to Seminary Park, from which the fences and also the benches had been removed. Mr. Saunders disputed with Mr. Ahearn on the assessment of the site, but Messrs.' Patchke and Jacobs, City Assessors, confirmed Mr. Ahern's figures.

The Warren Site Available

Assessor Patchke in a few words said that the Warrens site was very hilly and that made it valuable. It was centrally located, making it accessible. In answer to a question if it was level, he replied: "Quite level, when you get there." Mr. Pathcke pointed out that the other parks sites as proposed were some distance from the center of the city and that the Warren site was the only available site in the central park of the Troy.
Others in Favor of the Bill

Assessor Jacobs said he had intended to say nothing, but felt it incumbent on him, when the representative from his district was assailed, to speak a word. He said Mr. Ahern had been elected by a comfortable majority from a district which had previously been Democratic by 2,900. He favored the Warren Hill site on account of its natural fitness, its accessibility and central location.

Alderman Beattie and James McCabe also supported the Warren hill site. The hearing was then declared closed.

Favorably reported

The park bill was favorably reported in the Assembly this afternoon."

So it appears that even with opposition with the powerful Chamber of Commerce the bill moved forward. The local papers championed the idea of a park as this editorial suggests on February 15, 1901 in the Troy Daily Times:

"Park and Parks

The desire for parks in this city is so great that the question is not park or "no park" but "This park or the other one."

Assemblyman Ahern's bill is for the Warren Hill park – a splendid location for sightlines and accessibility. There is a strong sentiment in the central and southern parts of the city, and in the Fifth and adjacent wards, for this hill park, which can be secured now better than at any other time.

Assemblyman Galbraith favors the Waterworks Farm, already the property of the city and presenting fine opportunities for park cultivation. The northern part of the city, including Upper Troy – the former Lansingburgh – is friendly to the waterworks property. This site, it must be remembered, included the picturesque defile running from Oakwood Avenue to Glen Avenue, so that it would not be necessary to go to Oakwood Avenue before reaching the park. Development here would advance the value of a large area of neighboring property.

Troy is a long city. If the people at one end want a park, easily obtainable by the city, and if the people at the other end want a park, now the property of the city, why not both? Why not?

Assemblyman Ahern wants the Warren Hill Park established, but he has said repeatedly that he is not opposed to additional park facilities. Probably Assemblyman Galbraith is not averse to Warren Hill as an addendum. Why not both?"

On February 23 the Daily Times reported a petition drive:

"A petition was circulated yesterday to be presented to the Mayor in favor of a public park in the city and especially the Warren Hill site. Copies of the petition were placed in stores and business places throughout the city, and this morning a large number of names had been signed. The first copies were distributed along Congress Street on Ida Hill adjacent to the proposed park site."

The Mayor of Troy received a copy of the bill on March 1:

"A copy of Assemblyman Ahern's bill providing for a park on the Warren Hill site reached Mayor Conway at 11:40 o'clock this morning. A date for the public hearing has not yet been set."

Ten days later Mayor Conway had set up a public hearing for March 14th:

"A public hearing on the Warren Hill park bill, which has been passed by the Legislature, will be held Thursday evening at the City Hall by Mayor Conway and the Common Council."

The day before the Troy Daily Times outlined the battle:

"The Park Bill Favored
Troy Merchants and others express their opinions in relation to the Warren Hill site – Respond why the city should establish a park there – Is accessible and has many natural advantages. Much interest is manifested in the project for a public park for Troy, as embodied in the bill providing for the establishment of one on Warren hill. The bill, which was introduced in the Assembly by Assemblyman Ahearn, and which has passed both houses of the Legislature, is now in the hands of the Mayor. In accordance with the requirements of the law a hearing will be given by the Mayor and Common Council, the date having been set for to-morrow evening at 8 o'clock in the Common Council chamber. There is a strong sentiment in favor of the site provided for in the bill, as the expressions of opinion given below will show:
The Only Practical Plantation

W.W. Loomis said he was decidedly in favor of the Warren Hill for a park. "I think it is the only practical park scheme that has been offered to the city of Troy," he continued. "The waterworks property is all right for people who can afford to be continually paying car fare or for those owning horses, but for the poor people it is not to be compared with the Warren property. I don't object to the waterworks farm as a park for the benefit of the residents of the northern part of the city. I believe they are entitled to it and should have it. I am very much surprised at the dog-in-the-manger feeling exhibited by the people who favor that as against the Warren property.

"The chief argument brought to bear against the bill is the money that is to be spent; yet some people advocate the Edgerton system, which will cost the city $500,000. I fail to see that they are consistent. The Edgerton park scheme has been asleep for the last ten years, and would probably have slept forever if the park bill had not been introduced."

"The Chamber of Commerce opposed the Warren Park bill, but you don't hear a word out of them against the bill for a private driving park, or speedway, as it is called, which proposes to bond the city for $50,000. That's where they show their good sense. I am heartily in favor of the speedway, and if we spent a little more money in public improvements we would be a good deal better off. Give us the speedway, give us the waterworks farm for a park and give us Warren Hill for a park. We cannot have too many of those things."

The Most Desirable Place.

Andrew M. Church said he was much in favor of the Warren Hill site for a park. "The waterworks property is all right," he added, "but it is not good for our section of the city. I am in favor of the Warren property because it is from every standpoint the most desirable place."

Has Natural Advantages

Ex-school commissioner James Smyth said: "I don't know whether Warren Hill is the best place or not. I have said several times that it would be the easiest place to make into a park, because the trees and other natural advantages are already there. Still, I don't know whether it is the best place or not; there may be other good places."

Can Be Easily Reached

John B. Holmes said he was in favor of the Warren property for a park, and had been all the time. He thought it the most desirable place that had been suggested. Mr. Holmes gave as reason for favoring the site the following: "First, it is accessible to the largest number of people; second, there are a large number of trees, and it is ready to be occupied as a park. It can be reached from all parts of the city by the electric cars. These are a few reasons; there are many more which, in my opinion, are why it should be preferred."

A Fine View

Charles A. Evans expressed himself as much in favor of the bill for a park on the Warren property. "I know what the park is,: he said. "I am very much in favor of Warren's Hill for a park, and I am also in favor of a park for Upper Troy and one for the Iron Works district. Warren's Hill is a delightful place for the poor people to resort to for a breathing spot. It is the most beautiful place we can get. I played there when a boy, and know every foot of the ground. There is a beautiful view of the country for miles around, and the height about the city renders the air pure and invigorating. A park should not be for the rich and well to do, but for the people who are unable to go away during the summer and who need a breathing spot near at hand.

"I think the Warren Hill property is one of the best sites for the purpose in this section. There are high ground and good air, and the lookout from the top of the hill is one of the grandest sights in the valley. I would not make the place too exclusive, but would give plenty of room for a ground where the children can romp and play. We cannot have too many playgrounds for the children.

"I would go further; I am also in favor of Upper Troy having a park. Rensselaer Park and Young's Groove combined would make a good place. Also give the residents of lower Troy, the Iron Works district, a park on the hill in that section. The people who have the means and can go away with their families during the heated season and enjoy a change of air and climate do not need a park. But those who have to stay at home need just such a place as Warren's Hill would give them, a place to breathe."

The Question of Expense

"I am certainly in favor of parks for Troy," said William H. Shields, manager of the Griswold Wire Works. "The only question is as to location. Warren Hill has the advantage of central location, but it seems to me that the expense would be very great to put it in shape for a park. The county farm and waterworks property, with plenty of land adjoining, which could be purchased for much less money, could be made into parks to much better advantage. These sites also have the advantage of water, which can never be had at Warren Hill. This city certainly needs parks, and I know of no city which has more available sites for parks than Troy."

Should have a system of parks

Arthur G. Sherry, of the firm of Squires, Sherry & Galusha, stated that he held to the opinions which he "expressed some time ago. He said. "I believe we should have a comprehensive system of parks, including the Warren Hill site, the waterworks farm and several smaller parks. The parks should where they can reached by all the residents of the city."

Will beautify the City

Gen. C. Whitney Tillinghast, 2d, spoke in reference to the matter as follows: "I am now and always have been in favor of a park system. I am in favor of every public measure that will beautify the city and add to the comfort of its citizens. I believe Troy should be a modern city in every respect. No community is what it should be unless it has within its borders a well appointed hotel, a suitable theater, railroad conveniences of the best, a water supply, pure and plentiful; a public bath, if the situation will permit, and parks for the health, pleasure and comfort of its citizens. It seems to be the consensus of opinion that no more beautiful spot exists than Warren Hill, and if it can be purchased at a suitable price I favor that location. But I would not advocate paying even the assessed valuation. We have stood still, while our sister cities of the state have forged ahead.

"In private enterprises Trojans are energetic, farseeing and, as a rule, successful; but in public enterprises it seems almost an impossibility to obtain unselfish, energetic concert of action. They all declare that they want public improvements, but in the same breath throttle the scheme by objecting to the methods employed for obtaining it. To me the method seems immaterial. What I want is results, honestly and economically obtained. Much has been said about using the County House Farm, but that is not now feasible, as its title is vested in the County of Rensselaer. I certainly favor using any moneys available in immediately improving the waterworks property, looking toward making that one link in the chain of parks that should and, I believe, will finally exist."

The Best Location

James J. Campbell of 102 Congress Street expressed himself as much in favor of the proposed Warren Hill Park. "It is the only place in Troy suitable for a park," he said, "and in fact it is the *best location that could be secured. There are no shade trees at the waterworks site, which are so much needed. The Warren Hill property, with the Provincial Seminary property to the north, which may be purchased afterward and connected by a viaduct would make an ideal park. These sites are the only ones where shade trees are available, and which may be useful as a park to the present generation."*

For the Masses

P.A. Calder recalled other projects for parks in this city, and said he was strongly in favor of the Warren Hill site. He said:

"A good many years ago Mr. Adams of Adams Island fame gave me to understand that certain Alderman of Troy had endeavored to gain through legislation control of Adams Island for park purposes, and it was a serious grievance to him in his declining years that any one should seek to take from him property to which he had a just claim and right. However, that in my mind was the ideal location for a public park in Troy, because it had the advantages of nearly every qualification. It was very easily approached from every side. People of means could easily take a ferry at Broadway or other points and ride to the State dam, where another ferry or a bridge, which could easily be through across the branch of the Mohawk, would convey them to the park. The approaches to the park would be delightful. With the present railroad facilities any part of the island could be reached by car. There is no more delightful place in this vicinity that that and the scenery from the western approach is grand.

"Next to this site it would seem from its central location and beautiful views that the Warren property would be best. It has already nearly everything necessary for a park, and with the addition and improvements that would be made delightful in the extreme.

"The object of a public park is to benefit the masses, and certainly the smallest child would be able to walk to the Warren site without fatigue. The people who have means take a very early departure from the city to the county, and have but little use for a public park. And when the park reaches the glory of the summer they are not using it. When they return to the city with the falling leaves there is still no use to them for a park. To make poor people pay to visit and return from a park or to cause them to walk under the sweltering sun to reach an inaccessible spot does not seem to meet the idea of a park which is to be a benefit to the very persons who should have the benefit. It would cause them to be prostrated and utterly unfit to enjoy the beauties of the park when they arrived there. The Warren Hill site seems favorable on account of its central location and its easy access."

The afternoon edition of the paper went into more detail:

"The Legislature has passed a bill providing for a park on Warren Hill in this city. The bill will be before Mayor Conway to-morrow evening for a public hearing.

Warren Hill as a park is accessible. For people who do not own horses and carriages, and to whom the time and expense of a journey to a distant park would be prohibitory, the central location of Warren Hill is a strong argument in its favor. It would be a people's park, because the people could get to it and could enjoy it.

For conspicuousness and sightliness Warren Hill is unsurpassed if equaled. A park there would be a commanding feature, advertising the city to every traveler, and giving to citizen's landscape views of remarkable extent and diversity.

This is the time – and probably the only time – to get possession of this property for public purposes.

There have always been faultfinders who contended that Troy was not progressive enough in securing such public attractions as parks, and that there should be effective effort in this direction. Those who so believe must certainly lend their encouragement to a park movement which has done something and which has a tangible result, approved by the Legislature, to offer the people. The friends of the parks have an opportunity at hand.

The Warren Hill Park need not interfere with the development of other city property. But it will give a central, accessible, sightly hill park, which will be a nucleus for such other park development as the city may find desirable in future.

The Warren Hill Park is at hand. This is the time to speed it and not to delay it. Those who believe in parks for the people- in parks with popular characteristics – may well attend the public hearing at the City Hall to-morrow evening and array themselves on the side of progress."

Troy's City Hall on Third and State where the public hearing battles took place. Now Barker Park.

The results of the public hearing held at City Hall were covered in detail on March 15 in the Troy Daily Times:

"For Parks and Progresses

The result of the public hearing last evening on the Warren Hill Park bill was a victory for the element in this city that favors progress. It was a victory for parks for the people that is, for parks that, beautifully in themselves, add the decisive merit of accessibility by which alone can their beauty be made available to any considerable number of the city's population.

The local tribunal, consisting of the Mayor and Common Council, decided by a vote of 11 to 5 to approve the Warren Hill Park bill. All the Republican Alderman, with Mayor Conway and two Democratic Alderman, voted in favor of the bill.

The decision was reached after thoroughly canvassing the arguments.

The Principal objection was on the ground of expense. But Assemblyman Ahern, the introducer of the bill, answered that objection as it has always been answerable when any public improvement has been proposed, that the expense will be a distributed burden of which posterity shall bear its part, and that the individuals proportion will be so small as not to be considered as a counterpoise to the resulting advantage of a modern improvement in a modern city.

To the desire for the waterworks Farm as a public park, the answer was ready that the waterworks farm is now a city park, with a sum available each year for the development of the property. The county farm belongs to the county, and would need to be purchased like any other property.

The elevation of the hill, to which some objected, is its crowning recommendation. Every city that Nature has permitted to be built in a rolling country and not on the dead flat of a prairie puts its park on a hill. That is where a park belongs. A park is not a commercial or industrial plant, which must be located near a freight track or a waterway navigated by merchant vessels. As engineer Baltimore pointed out, the elevation gives opportunity for the winding ascents which multiply the beauties of such a park.

It is scarcely to be disputed that the reason why the Warren bill was not included in the system of parks suggested a number of years ago what that it was known that during Dr. Warrens' lifetime his cottage and grounds, dear to his heart, were not and would not be for sale. His death, and the termination of use by the Warren family of the property as a place of personal residence, left the possibility of its acquirement by the public.

The statements by the Mayor and the Aldermen who favored affirmative action on the bill were convincing in their presentation of arguments. Alderman Barnes said the place was already a park with beautiful drives. Alderman Breckenridge pointed out the central location and therefore supreme accessibility.

Mayor Conway summarized the situation when he said: the site is beautiful, available and in the center of the city. The majority of the people favor its acquisition. The present administration is pledged by the people's vote to such improvement as waterworks and parks. If the old democratic administration had done its duty toward waterworks and parks, both would not have been left as a legacy of unperformed obligation for the city of to-day to take up. The bill does not make it obligatory to pay an excessive sum for the property, and does not commit the city to any specific expenditure. The Mayor's summing up as to the lands on Warren Hill is so well judged and sensible that it will commend itself to both the enterprise and the discretion of the city: "I think they are adapted for a public park. I think they should be utilized by the city of Troy for that purpose. If they can purchased for a fair price by the city of Troy I shall advocate the taking of these premises for a public park."

Last night's hearing on the park question was progressive, and was a victory for clear views on an elevated plane."

In the same paper was this:

"Last night's hearing made one thing very evident – the sentiment in favor of parks for Troy is overwhelming, even though there be some differences of opinion as to sites."

The afternoon edition of the Daily Times added:

"The Bill Approved For Warren Hill Park

The Mayor and common council after a hearing endorse Assemblyman Ahern's measure- a large attendance – opposition from the chamber of commerce – arguments in favor of the proposition – the city's need – how the Aldermen voted.

Mayor Conway and the Common Council last evening formally approved Assemblyman Ahern's measure know as the Warren Hill Park bill. The action was taken at the conclusion of one of the most largely attended and most enthusiastic hearings ever held in the city. Every ward was represented and a great diversity of opinion was shown. Petitions with thousands of names for and against the measure were submitted. The park question was discussed in all phases. Notwithstanding the fact that there were seats of only a small number in the Common Council Chamber, where the hearing was held, was packed to the doors, and many belated persons stood in the corridors to hear the words of the speakers.
Inauguration of a Park System

The Principal opposition was from the Chamber of Commerce, its Committee on Public Improvements, in accordance with a resolution, being present to speak against the measure. During the evening, however, the sentiment was expressed that the approval of the measure was really the starting point of a system of parks for the city, and with that idea in view much of the bitterness of the opposition faded and the result of the hearing was received with a great delight. The hearing continued, with a short recess, from 8:20 o'clock until 11 o'clock. Interest, *however was so great that during the entire session every available place was occupied, men standing the windows and settees, or sitting on the floor.*

Beginning the Hearing

Long before 8 o'clock the chamber was crowded. The Democratic members of the Common Council occupied their seats early, and the Republicans arrived shortly after 8 o'clock. Mayor Conway and President Closson occupied seats on the platform, the former presiding at the hearing. In calling the meeting to order Mayor Conway said:

"Gentlemen: this meet of the city and its legislative body is called for the purpose of giving a hearing on the bill known as the Warren Park bill and entitled "an Act to provide for the acquisition and improvement by the city of Troy of certain lands for public parks purposes" The Mayor directed the Clerk to call the roll. Alderman Breckenridge and Alderman Larkin were absent. Mr. Breckenridge, who had recently been ill arrived later and took his seat. The Mayor then submitted proofs of publication of the notices of the hearing and Clerk Lecomte read the text of the bill. The Mayor then declared the hearing open, and invited any to speak who desired to be heard on the subject. He stated that the opposition would be heard first.

The Chamber of Commerce

President William F. Gurley of the Chamber of Commerce was the first speaker. He said he was present with other members of the Committee on Public Improvements as a result of the action of the Chamber of Commerce at its recent public meeting, when this committee had been instructed to oppose the measure. He continued:

"We are here not to oppose in an unreasonable way the subject of public parks or public improvements. We wish it thoroughly understood that the committee and the Chamber of Commerce are here in favor of public parks and believe them to be along the lines of a modern city. We believe that every city should have parks for the comfort and pleasure of its people. We are not here to oppose a systematic and well developed plan for public parks in Troy. But we do believe, and are here to why we so believe, that parks, as already planned – one in the northern and one in the southern section of the city, and on land that the city already owns or is in a great measure of possession – are to be preferred to the proposition presented here tonight in this bill. And why? It is simply and purely a business question. We feel that the expense which a park on Warren Hill will involve would much better direct in the development of the parks already practically in our possession, with a boulevard connecting. I will introduce Mr. Don, Chairman of the committee.

Caution Counseled

Mr. Don spoke briefly and to the point as follows:

"The question of public parks is one that should have careful and intelligent consideration, and inasmuch as a former Park Commission has given the subject a great deal of thought and study, and an expert engineer on public parks was employed them to lay out a system of parks which was approved by the Commission, but was not put in force owning to conditions which they could not control, it would seem wise that the bill now pending to acquire possession of Warren Hill should be at least discontinued until next winter, and the system of parks, as laid out by Mr. Edgerton and the Commission, should be taken up and thoroughly analyzed, eliminating any of the objectionable features that might be found, but still might have the nucleus of a good system of parks.

The cost of the Warren Hill property should be taken into consideration. From what has been published in the newspapers, from an authoritative source, it would indicate that the price named in the bill (which was considered by many people as too high) would be sufficient to purchase this property. This is a very important matter for the people of Troy.

A Commission Suggested

We are all in favor of public parks to have them located in the most favorable section for the benefit of the entire city, and would suggest to your honor that you might appoint a Park Commission and give them such powers as you may deem wise, and have them report to you at a given time.

There is decided opposition to the Warren Hill project by many of our citizens and there are those in favor of it, and if you think favorably of the above suggestion it would seem that it might assist in arriving at some conclusion that would bring about harmony of action, and in the near future have a system of parks that would be a benefit to our citizens and a credit to our city.

Favored the Edgerton Scheme

J.W. Donnelly outlined the work of the Chamber of Commerce Committee on Public improvements saying that the member had given much attention to the subject. Warren Hill was an excellent location for a park, but was not available for the purpose. On account of its declivities and ravines only about half of the acreage could be utilized for park purposes. If $160,000 was to be expended for so small a plat it would mean a very large sum for a park system in Troy. The site could never be a real park, for the water facilities would be lacking. On the other hand, the waterworks property was already a natural park. Beautiful water and landscape effect were already there, trees were growing and the site was ideal. Under the Edgerton system of a north and south park with a connecting boulevard the value of surrounding property would enhanced, beautiful buildings would spring up and the expense would be offset by the increased tax revenue to the city. On the contrary, the property adjacent to Warren Hill was already occupied, and could not be so enhanced in value.

Mr. Donnelly showed from measures passed in the Legislature in 1892 that the waterworks site and the county house property could easily be obtained by the city for park purposes. Indeed in the former case the Speaker was of the opinion that the opening of the waterworks farm was merely a formal proceeding, the duty falling the Commissioner of Public Works. He said that the expenditure of $15,000 a year, as authorized under the White charter, would put this land in fine condition for a park, and there would be no burden on the taxpayers. On the contrary, the Warren Hill Park would involve a large expenditure. The Speaker emphasized his approval of the Edgerton plan, and declared it was a matter for serious consideration. He said that Warren Hill was not easy of access on account of its steep sides, and styled an approach to the hill as a heart breaking climb.

Mr. Ahern said Warren Hill was 120 feet high and the waterworks property 370 feet. Mr. Donnelly said that might be true, but the approach to the waterworks property was an easy and gradual ascent. He styled the view from Warren Hill as one of the housetops and chimneys and concluded by exhorting all to cast aside prejudice and work for the interest of Greater Troy.

Views of an Architect

E.W. Loth also a member of the Chamber of Commerce, said there seem to be no division of sentiment as to whether or not Troy ought to have parks. He said the Warren Hill site would benefit perhaps 10,000, and questioned where the other 60,000 would come in. He said that from any point in this vicinity a Trojan might point to Warren Hill and say, "There's our park." Could that be done in New York in the case of Central Park, in Boston in the case of the Commons or the public gardens in Albany? Assuredly not. The elevation is not a necessary factor in a park site. Troy had paid, the speaker said, for the views of an expert. He had reported on a scheme that was feasible several years ago, and much more so now that Lansingburgh had been annexed – for the reason that the waterworks property would be central for the northern section. The Warren Hill site was small in comparison with the proposed beautiful sites in the north and south ends. A boulevard could be constructed and soon Troy's park system would be the best in the country. The speaker counseled following up a well established plan instead of going at the subject haphazard and taking a bit here and bit there without any continuity or connection. The Edgerton system the speaker said, would be a monument to Troy.

On a Business Basis.

H.S. McLeod said when it was realized that Troy would be a city eighty five years old within a few weeks it was certain that the time had arrived for parks. The subject ought to be attacked. A commission ought to be appointed or something done to obtain them. On the other hand, the steps ought to be taken with care and economy. The work should be established on an economic basis. Troy's scenery was equal, the speaker said, to any in the state. He thought it would be well and best to being the system by developing the land which was already owned by the city.

Ten Missions Represented

President Hurley said the committee had reason to believe that there were other citizens and large taxpayers who were of the same idea as the Chamber of Commerce. He submitted petitions opposing the measure to which were attached something over 1200 names representing $10,000,000 assessed valuation.
Question and Replies

Mr. Barnes asked Mr. Gurley if he could state what proportion of the Chamber of Commerce was opposed to the measure, saying he knows of some who favored the Warren site. Mr. Gurley replied that he could not say, but at a public meeting called or the purpose of considering the question the action had been unanimous, and the meeting had been attended by about 125 persons. Mr. Gurley said ten or perhaps twelve letters had been received by the Chamber of Commerce from members who were in favor of the measure.
Mr. Barne's asked if parks would be an inducement to business concerns to locate in Troy. Mr. Gurley replied that any improvement which tended to beautify the city or enhance the comfort of the citizens counted in the city's favor.

Scorned Public Officials

L.H. Ryan of the Eight Ward spoke against parks in general and denounced public officials. He declared that parks were the congregating places of vagrants and hoodlums.

History of Troy's Parks

J.S. Saunders opposed the measure because of its expense. He said it was evident that the people of Troy were interested in the question as the attendance showed. The object of parks was to give a breathing space to the people of a city. He said other cities went in the suburbs for their parks, and cited Buffalo, Baltimore, Albany and other places as examples. He said adjourning property was thus enhanced in value, and the increased revenue would pay all the expenses of a park. The speaker referred to the various propositions for parks in the city, and declared that Troy might have been well supplied with parks if gifts which had been offered had been accepted. He quoted from reports that expense of land for parks in their cities, and drew a conclusion that but about thirty acres of land in the Warren site were fit for a park. He said that meant an expenditure of more than $5000 an acre for the Warren Site. He declared that $160,000 would build an electric railroad from Troy to the Grafton Mountain and would transport the citizens free every day in the week to the Grafton Mountains. This sum of money was too great to be expended on a small site like the Warren proper. He closed with the question addressed to the Mayor and Common Council: "When we need waterworks and so many other improvement, can you allow this useless expenditure of money for a small site?"

Too Extravagant a Project

Alderman Hogan said that he did not wish to discuss the good and bad points of the Warren site, but had did desire to say that if the city should acquire the Warren property for a park it would be inadequate. It may be said that it will do until we get something better. It is a beautiful spot, and that's all there was of it. The speaker said it was not more accessible than the waterworks property which could easily be developed by the expenditure of the amount allowed under the charter. The waterworks property was easy of access, while Warren Hill was very steep and even dangerous to ascent. While the Warren site might be fairly good was not such as to warrant the expenditure of such an amount. The speaker had attended the meeting of the Chamber of Commerce, though he was not a member, and had coincided with its views. "The city is six miles long" said the Alderman. "Why take so small a portion for a park, which would need much money to place it in shape, when we have the waterworks property in the north and available land on the south? The opening of the waterworks property would open nearly every cross street in upper Troy. The development of the almshouse property would open main streets in the southern wards. This would benefit a large section of the city, while Warren Hill won't open a single street." The speaker explained how the judicious expenditure of $160,000 over a term of years would benefit the working classes. He even counseled spending more if the larger parks were opened, and said it would result in betterment to the city. He noted the expense of the waterworks, soon to be installed, the paving in upper Troy and many other improvements and said that it would be unwise to spend so much for so little.

For the Waterworks Property

Assemblyman Galbraith of the First District of Rensselaer County said that when the bill was before the Assembly he retarded its progress long enough to state his opposition. He believed there was need of a park in Troy, but as a business man believed in utilizing first the property already in the city's possession. He thought, however, if arrangement were made to open the waterworks property for a park and thus satisfy the residents of the upper city, that opposition to the Warren site would disappear. He thought, however, that the waterworks property should be utilized first because the city owned it. He concluded: "I contend, Mr. Mayor, that you owe it to the upper part of the city to open the waterworks property for park. It will do for Upper Troy what Warren Hill will do for the southern section. I understand that you have the power to do so. I appear not so much in opposition to this measure as in favor of the waterworks property for a park."

Favoring the Measure

Mayor Conway declared the hearing on the opposition closed at 9:50 o'clock and invited those to speak who desired to be heard in favor of the measure. Assemblyman Ahern, who was prominent on the floor, spoke briefly on the measure and introduced Ex-Assistant City Engineer Garnett D. Baltimore. The speaker is an experienced park engineer, having done much work at

Glens Falls, Amsterdam, Brattleboro, VT, Johnstown, Gloversville and in the Forest Park Cemetery in this city. His remarks follow.

"Ancient Troy, made immortal by the genius of Homer, was celebrated for its Mount Ida. Modern Troy is afforded the opportunity by the instrumentality of the bill before you tonight to acquire its Mount Ida as a place of recreation for Trojans. It is not my purpose to dwell upon the educational value of parks nor to discuss in detail the measure before you. That task will be assigned to those who are more eloquent. It is simply to call attention of the possibilities of the site selected from the landscape engineer's point of view. Warren Hill includes practically all the territory lying west of Marshall Street, south of Congress and Ferry Streets, east of the railroad and St Mary's Avenue and north of Hill Street. Included in the circle described within a radius of a mile is all that potion of the city north of Thompson Street, east of the river, south of Hoosick Street and west of Collins Avenue. Forty four thousand of our population are within that circle. Within the mile and one quarter radius are 50,000 or two thirds of the population of our entire city. There is no other site, sir, as central to do great a number of our people or as accessible to congested sections of our population.

Entrances can be established on the north at the junction of Congress Street near Thirteenth Street; on the east at Marshall Street on the west at Short Seventh Street and the dead of Liberty Street; on the south from several places on Hill Street while those who prefer the trolley can be brought from any section of our city to the entrances on the north. The plateau or elevated section of Warren Hill contains about forty acres of land, well wooded, rolling and varying. There is a section practically level west of the Vail Mansion, containing from ten to fifteen acres, that could treated as a mall. East of the Vail residence is a depression which could easily be converted into a lake of four or five acres in extent. There is no point in the ground where water could not be furnished by the City department. There are many opportunities for fine and effective landscape work. The eastern slope is composed of clay and gravel overlying a bed of rock. The general treatment here should be terracing, reinforced by retaining walls. Winding roads and paths with easy grades can be located, thus making the plateau accessible.

The Cost

The amount thus expended by the city of Troy for parks is comparative small compared with other cites, as the following with show:

Olmsted, the greatest authority on landscape treatment in the country today looks over a piece of ground and marks out is adaption and special effects. This the style motive of a park. The location of Warren Hill is unique, a bold promontory jutting out and extending over the city it stands like a sentinel guarding the valley of the Hudson, revealing a landscape of miles in extent and extraordinary beauty. To the south, the eye follows the windings and turnings of the Hudson, dotted with craft, until it reaches Albany, with its capitol silhouette against the blue outlines of the Helderbergs and Catskills. To the west, the city at your feet, teeming with life and industry, the river spanned by its bridges, Watervliet, the Arsenal and on and on until the horizon kisses the distance hills. To the north, Waterford, Cohoes and on until the view melts into hazy distance. To the east, one looks on until the blue mountains of Grafton stop the vision. Hence the Motive.

I pity from the bottom of my heart the man who, standing on the brow of Warren Hill at sunset and gazing upon the panorama of life and beauty, tinted by all the golden beams of a declining sun, can see only in that vista the chimneys and tops of buildings. On the contrary, such a vision should be an incentive to youth, an inspiration to manhood and solace to old age.

Compared With Brussels.

A.J Weise, who is the author of "Troy's One Hundred Years" and other works of local history, spoke at some length. In opening he compared the city with Brussels, and spoke of the park advantage there and the similarity of one of the most desirable parks with that which the Warren Hill property would make possible. He styled the idea of a park to be of educational interest to children – a place for them to have recreation, fresh air, fun, games, to get acquired with one another and to learn to associate one with another. He declared that almost any time on a summer day the children could be found playing in remote parts of the grounds, and declared that they would not go there unless there were attractions for them. He dwelt on the beauties of the hill and the superb view. He pointed out that in years gone by the hill had been famed for its beauty. That the appellation of Mount Ida had been given it because the name was fitting, patterned after the old Mount Ida of fame. He questioned if it were will to wait fifty years longer and pay twice as much for the property of 100 years and pay four times as much. Better, he said to have purchased it thirty years ago for half the sum. The speaker predicted that a park on the Warren Hill site would make a change in the buildings on Congress Street and other adjoining property, and that the enhanced value of property would be the same in this case as in the other sites. He thought the site could be made picturesque and beautiful in a short time. He counseled its selection because it was already a natural park and would be ready within a few month's time for actual use. In conclusion, he said if this opportunity were allowed to pass Troy would not have a park in fifty years.

Introduce the Bill

Assemblyman Ahern was the next speaker favoring the bill. He said that he had the honor of introducing the measure in the Assembly January 14 of this year. It was published in all of the papers, and there had been a public hearing on the measure at Albany before the Assembly committee. A committee from the Chamber or Commerce had opposed the measure. Mr. Ahern said he was familiar with the waterworks and the almshouse property and that they were desirable sites. Yet neither would supply the place of need which would be satisfied by the Warren Hill site. He spoke of former legislation in the common council in which he had been interested and touched on the subject of removing Mount Olympus, which he's styled as "an unsightly piece or rock." He declared if it was in his district he would have a bill providing for its removal from the city. Mr. Ahern opposed the idea of a north and south park with a connecting boulevard, if the boulevard necessitated a bridge or viaduct across the Poesetenkill 100 feet above water on the ground that an expense of $250,000 for the bridge would not be economy. He said he was in favor of parks and all public improvements.

For the People

Mr. Ahern recited the history of the bill and stood sponsor for it. He declared that his measure never intended that the full price of $160,000 should be paid for the Warren property. He thought it would cost much less. He noted the assessments on the property, however, and said if the property was not worth what it was assess for then the city had been robbing the Warren Estate for years. Mr. Ahern said he was always willing to do his duty, and in introducing this measure he was working for the people. In relation of the proposed expensive masonry needed for retaining walls he thought much of the expense could be avoided by proper planting of trees and grass. He noted that if the props were pulled from a house it would fall. Consequently it was not a wonder that when people had dug the sand and earth from the under of Warren Hill that here had been a landslide. If it would be dangerous as a park it was dangerous now, and the city ought to see that it is cared for. Mr. Ahern said that when the fireworks were displayed from Starbucks Island some years ago, 5000 people were on Warren Hill to witness them. That, he said, provided that the location was central. It showed the desire of the people to go there and the natural fitness of the hill for a public park. Mr. Ahern concluded by explaining the financing of the measure and was accorded warm applause. He also filed a number of petitions, signed, he said, by taxpayers and rent payers. There were more than 6,000 names attached.

A short recess

Upon the application of Mr. Barnes the Mayor granted a recess of fifteen minutes to allow a perusal of the petitions. After the recess the Mayor declared to the hearing closed. He directed the Clerk to call the roll, and during the roll a number of the Republican Alderman took occasion to explain their votes.

A Natural Park

Alderman Barnes said that when the matter first came up he had favored the waterworks site, but upon visiting the Warren Hill site had wondered how many of the men who had signed petitions against the measure had ever been on that hill. He contained in part:

"It is already a park. There are drives and trees and walks, and finer view I never saw. The residents of the hill tell me that the temperature is always from two to five degrees cooler than the lower part of the city. It is a model park – could be made an actual park by simply placing benches at intervals. There are eight buildings on the property which could utilized. The Warren building is a beautiful place and would make a fine waiting room or museum. We know that the

Chamber of Commerce is a body of men who desire to advance the interests of the city. They have met with some successes, but is up hill work because the city is about thirty years behind. Compared with other cities of the second class Troy shows no gain. We have Monument Square, the Court House, and the Seminary buildings to show our friends, the only other place of interest is the city of the dead on the hill. And I am inclined to think that Troy is in keeping with that city. We will soon have waterworks and they will be self sustaining. Therefore that expense should not be figured in the taxes. A park system is a thing to be desired and the tax will be but a trifle. And is with the understanding that this Warren Hill is but the beginning of a park system of the city I heartily vote in favor.

A Good Start

Mr. Breckenridge spoke briefly saying that he had hoped to see the waterworks property owned, and that when this bill was first presented he was not in favor of it. He had thought that the waterworks, the new depot, the paving and improvements in the city should have the first attention. Careful consideration had shown him that Warren property was a desirable start thus he was heartily in favor of it, with the understanding that the waterworks property would soon be transform into a park.

Hopes to see More Smokestacks

Mr. Beattie was in favor of a park, and hoped that the view would soon embrace more smokestacks and indications of additional business and manufacture.

Troy's New Era

Mr. Dauchy thought that now was the time, if a beginning was to be made. Through the efforts of the Mayor a new and fine depot was assured. The waterworks was an assured fact. Now a park system was near, and if these improvements were augmented by others he felt sure that the next census would show improved returns for Troy.

Time to stop fighting

Mr. McMurray was not heartily in favor of the Warren Hill site, but he declared it unwise to keep fighting, one section against another, about the location of a park, with the certain result that there would none at all. He hope to see the waterworks property developed soon
He voted in favor of the bill.

Vote of the Aldermen

Clerk Lecomte called the roll and the votes were as follows;

In favor – Messrs. 'Atkins, Barnes, Beattie, Breckenridge, Burke, Casey, Dauchy, Fradenburgh, Gray, McMurray and Spence.

Opposed – Messrs. 'Cahill, Hogan, O'Brien, Purcell, and Tracey.

The Mayors Approval

When Mayor Conway was called upon to approve or veto the bill he made a brief address, defining his position as follows:

Mr. Clerk: In voting upon the question before the meeting I desire to make the following statement:

This project to acquire Warren Bill for a public city park has been very widely discussed, and it is apparent that there is a great difference of opinion upon the subject. The lands selected for a public park by the provisions of this bill are the most beautiful and sightly in the city of Troy. Nature has done all that it is possible to do for these lands, and for the purpose of a city park they are the most beautiful and the only available land in the midst of the city that could be selected.

There is no question in my mind but that they are preeminently fitted for the uses of a public park. I do not believe that any one will gainsay this. Moreover, while there is a great difference of opinion on the subject, I believe that a majority of the people favor the acquisition of the lands for park purposes. I do not know that it is possible to establish such a proposition positively, but as far as I can learn from inquirers made and from the speech of people I believe this to be the fact.

Administration Pledge

The present administration came into office pledged to give to the people of the city of Troy certain improvement, and among them public parks, and the majority of our citizens now insist that they are entitled to all those public comforts and convenience which are provided by modern and progressive cities.

If the improvements provide for by the public park bill of 1892 and the water bill of 1894 had been made in former years, when they ought to have been made, the city of Troy would now be in the position and condition of having everything at once in the line of progress and improvement forced upon it. But this is a condition which confronts us, and we must meet it. We must do what possible for the city and its people, and what will prove of some benefit to themselves.

The waterworks property should be developed gradually under the provisions of the law of 1892 by small annual expenditures. The city owns this land, and I see no reason why the city should not in a few years have a public park in the neighborhood of its beautiful lakes.

But I also think it practical and advisable to utilize the Warren Hill as a public park, and as contemplate by this act, provided it can be purchased for a reasonable sum of money. This bill provides for the expenditure of $160,000. I do not think that price should give for the Warren Hill property, and I shall not be in favor of paying any such sum for these premises. I think they are adapted for a public park. I think they should be utilized by the city of Troy for that purpose. If they can be purchased at a fair price by the city of Troy I shall advocate the taking of these premises for a public park. Thus far I am willing to go, and upon these lines I am ready and willing to accept and approve this proposed measure.

Accordingly I vote aye for its adoption and approval.

To be Returned to the Legislature

Mayor Conway stated that the result of the proceedings was that the Mayor and the Common Council had accepted the measure and that he should return the bill so certified to the Legislature. The hearing was concluded shortly after 11 o'clock.

On March 20, the Chamber of Commerce had their annual meeting and continued the dialogue about the creation of parks and their continued objection to Prospect Park:

"*Message from Chamber of Commerce Annual meeting*

For Public Parks

We believe one of the needed improvements in our city is a system of public parks. We have advocated strenuously the decision arrived at by the Public Improvement Committee and approved unanimously by a general meeting of this body.

A site not favored by us was selected but we believe so earnestly in at least a beginning of a park system that we trust that Warren Hill may be so converted and improved that the park thus situated may be a benefit to our people, and by convincing us what we have missed by years of inaction it will stimulate the extension of the park system along the lines favored by the former Park Commission.

Improvements along broad lines should be carried through, and will inevitably benefit the community and increase its standing throughout the country. On these grounds we advocate the elimination of grade crossings. The bill recently passed for fine roads in Rensselaer County is another move along the lines of public progress and should be heartily commended."

On March 26 the paper recorded the signing of the park bill into law: *"Governor Odell signed the Warren Hill Park Bill."*

Now that the bill was signed it was still up to the city to negotiate with the Warren estate to try and get a good price for the land. People were eager to visit the Mount Ida site and thought the land was going to be open for public inspection but on April 8th the Times posted this:

"Agent W.W. Rousseau of the Warren Estate stated to-day that the Warren Hill grounds would not be thrown open to the public on the Sundays during this month to allow people to inspect the site. He said that as agent he had received no official notice of any action with reference to Warren Hill as a proposed park site, nor had permission been sought for the opening of the grounds for inspection.

The Chamber of Commerce continued to make its opposition to the park known as late as April 11:

"The bill for the appropriation of $400,000 to purchase lands

The Committee on Public Improvement (Chamber) held two meetings, appeared in the City Hall before the Mayor and Common Council in opposition of the Warren Hill Park bill and appeared before a representative of the United States War Department in a public hearing at Albany in advocacy of certain improvements in the Hudson River channel opposite Troy.

On the 25th of March the Troy Daily Times announced the deal:

"For a City park

Mayor Conway, Corporation Counsel Fagan, City Engineer Cary and Attorney George B. Wellington, the latter representing the Warren estate, this afternoon visited the Warren Hill park site, the waterworks property and other points on the hill with a view of discussing the matter of a public park for the city. Mayor Conway announced this afternoon that negotiations are pending for the purchase of property for the contemplated public park.

The following day it became official:

"A New Park For Troy

By an agreement entered into in a conference yesterday between Mayor Conway, Corporation Counsel Fagan and the heirs and legal representatives of the estate of N.B. Warren & Brothers, the city, for the price of $110,000, will come into possession of Warren Hill for the purposes of a public park.

The need for a public park of ample size, and easily accessible to those who will most appreciated and enjoy the park facilities, has long been evident in this city. The law which permitted the city to acquire Warren Hill for park purposes was an expression of the public desire for some breathing spot and place of recreation near the center of the city's population. The bill was indefatigably pushed by Assemblyman Ahern and was approved by the city authorities and by the people of Troy. The object of the bill has now been achieved, and Troy will be in possession of a public park superior in natural facilities and resources and convenient to the uses of the people.

The acquirement is made at a sum which is so moderate that the purchase cannot fail to meet the approbation of the people as a good business transaction. The sum to be paid, $110,000 is about $30,000 less than the assessed valuation of the property for years back, and is a still greater reduction from the price originally desired by the owners of the property. The sum permitted by the park law to be paid was $160,000. To Mayor Conway much credit is due for the sagacious way in which he guarded the interests of the city by refusing to put the measures of the park law into final operation until the time had arrived when a bargain could be made which was advantageous to Troy. The Mayor has steadfastly refused all propositions to take the land by condemnation, as that would have compelled the payment of the assessed valuation - $138,500.

The new park has about forty acres of tableland, and with the elevation of the area constitutes one of the most sightly parks in the United States. There is room enough on this highland, with its imposing view and its diversity of wooded and open land, for just the public playground of which Troy stands sadly in need. There is no place where the boys and youth of Troy can resort for sport. All who are interested in the moral and physical development of the boys of the city have complained that there is no place to which the boys can go for play. The streets alone are the present playground of Troy, and from them the police regulations debar the youths. The opening of this public park in a convenient place will provide room for grounds for such sports as baseball, football, tennis, croquet and other athletic games of the field, and there is room for a lake or sufficient size to form a large park for skating in the winter season. With provision for such summer and winter sports outdoors and for bank concerts, fireworks, and other public entertainments at various seasons of the year Troy will be in possession of a park and playground combined for which the people have longed for years, and which other cities of similar wealth and size have provided as among the chief necessities of a municipality. The magnificence of the view and the attractiveness of the elevated area with is space for rest and recreation will make this a breathing spot of which the people may be proud.

With the park on Warren Hill, the speedway and the new schoolhouse which will be provided in the Fourth Ward, Troy's public record of improvement for 1902 will be conspicuous for its excellence and permanent quality.

The Troy Times, which has steadfastly advocated the purchase at reasonable terms of Warren Hill for a public park, believes that this act on the part of the city authorities, already approved in advance by the Legislature of the state and by the people of the city in their official and unofficial capacity, will be accepted with gratification by Trojans. The possibilities of such a park in the future of the city as a means of health, recreation, entertainment and therefore general prosperity, are easily perceptible. Let the people unite in enthusiastic, intelligent and suggestive effort to second the purpose of the city authorities to make the park just as full of opportunity for the healthy, reasonable and decorous enjoyment of the people as it can possible become. With a new park, a new hotel and a new railroad station, Troy will certainly be taking a long step forward.

Welcome to the new city park for Troy!"

The afternoon edition of the paper added some more information to the story:

"A New Park for this City.

Warren Hill Purchased

The city and the Warren Heirs agree on the purchase for $110,000 of Warren Hill for a public park – The price nearly $30,000 less than the assessed valuation – Mayor Conway's patience rewarded – An amicable agreement reached - The sum agreed upon is $30,000 less than the amount named in the park bill – Admirable adapted to the public use -The provisions of the law – The legal steps to be taken.

Warren Hill will be a city park of Troy. The transfer of the property from the Warren estate to the city was agreed upon yesterday at a conference between Henry Warren, representing the Warren heirs; George B. Wellington, their attorney, and Mr. Camp of New York as business manager of the estate, on one side, and Mayor Conway and Corporation Counsel Fagan, in behalf of the city.

The Price

The price agreed upon is $110,000, and there is to be no additional allowance to the estate for expenses.

The Mayors Patience Rewarded

To secure for the sum of $110,000 this valuable property in the heart of the city will be generally conceded to be a good bargain for Troy, as it is nearly $30,000 less than the assessed valuation.

The bill introduced by Assemblyman Ahern, and approved by the city's authorities and by municipal sentiment, providing for the purchase of the Warren property for a city park, made that purchase discretionary with the city authorities. Under his discretion Mayor Conway has awaited the time when the purchase could be made to the best advantage. The price asked by the representatives of the Warren estate when the bill was passed was higher than the city was willing to pay. It was then intimated that the city might be forced by a suit at law to purchase the property. The Mayor, after consultation with the Corporation Counsel, decided that legal action could be begun only by the city, and no attention was paid to the suggestion that suit might be begun from the other side. To take the property by condemnation proceedings would have involved paying by the city of at least as much as the assessed value of the property, on which value the owners were paying taxes. This value was $138,500 and Mayor Conway believed the property could be purchased for less money. If condemnation proceedings had been resorted to the city could not very well have said that the property was worth less than the valuation at which the city itself had placed the estate. That valuation was $135,500, making with some additional lots on Ferry Street, a total of $138,500. In 1889 the assessed valuation of the estate was $146,000.

By the agreement entered into yesterday, however, the city secures this property, valued at one time by the city at $146,000 and later at $138,500 for $110,000, which is a reduction very creditable to the efforts of Mayor Conway, and to his sagacity and determination in waiting for the proper time to buy instead of being forced into a hasty purchase and therefore a greater expenditure on the part of the city.

The Property

The property which will come into possession of the city by the purchase of Warren Hill includes seventy acres. Of this area sixty acres are in the First Ward, four and one half acres of which are occupied by the Mount Ida Cottage, and ten acres are in the Eighth Ward. The assessed valuation put upon the property at present is:

Mount Ida Cottage with four and a half acres.........$42,500

Fifty -Five and half acres, First Ward.........$91,000

Ten Acres, Eighth Ward...........$2000

Total $146,000

In addition to the property on which this valuation was placed the city acquires for the $110,000 lots on Ferry Street of the estimated value of $3000, which will provide an entrance from that street to the park.

The Buildings

Besides the land there are two large buildings on the grounds – the Mount Ida Cottage, which is an elegant edifice formerly occupied by Dr. Nathan B. Warren, and the Vail House. Most of the land belonging to the Warren Cottage plat was formerly part of the D.T. Vail property, and his summer residence is also one of the buildings on the grounds. These two buildings can be utilized for waiting rooms, museums, keeper's lodge or any other purpose properly pertaining to a public park.

The park is principally an elevated plateau, the extent of which would surprise those who have never visited the place, and it is admirable adapted, from its magnificent outlook and from the character of the area of tableland, to the purposes of a public place of recreation. The Mount Ida Cottage property belongs to the Mary Warren Free Institute, having been bequeathed to that society in the will of the late Dr. Warren. The remainder of the property belongs to the family heirs of the Warren estate, one of the principal legatees being Henry Warren, who was in the city yesterday and who participated in the conference with the city authorities.

The Legal Proceedings

The Corporation Counsel will take the necessary legal proceedings to obtain title to the land. It is likely that these proceedings will take the form of condemnation through a public commission, in order that all the proceedings may be conducted in the most public way, but it is agreed that the owners of the property shall not put in a claim of value exceeding $110,000. The property when acquired will be under the supervision of the Department of Public Works of the city.

Public Improvements

With the new park on Warren Hill, the Speedway for which the bill has just been passed by the Legislature and the new school facilities in the Fourth Ward (School 5), the year 1902 will represent a large advance by the city in improvements for the comfort and instruction of the people, and will be a year to which the municipal administration can point with gratification and pride

The Park Law.

The law under which the property is acquired as follows:
(Not reproduced here).

Mayor Conway Views

Mayor Conway said to-day: "I have realized that the people of Troy desire to continue the work of public improvement, pledged to which I was elected Mayor more than two years ago. In obedience to their desire and to my pledge, the new waterworks system has been inaugurated and has already secured the city against a recurrence of the water famines which had distressed the eastern portion of Troy and which had interfered with manufacturing operations. The use of the Quackenkill water system and the completion of the preliminaries toward the introduction of the Tomhannock system have fulfilled the pledge which was made that Troy would be given a pure and ample water supply.

"Next to the new water supply I believe that the need and desire for a public park has been most keenly felt by citizens. That desire found expression in the bill passed by the Legislature, and approved by the city authorities and by citizens of all political parties, which provided for the acquisition by the city of Warren Hill for a public park. The price first asked by the owners of the property was greater that I felt the people of Troy would be willing to pay. If condemnation proceeding had been summarily entered upon, as some proposed and desired, the city would have been compelled to stand by its own valuation of the property, $138,500, which was only a little less than the owners asked for. Moreover, the city would have been obliged to pay the expenses of the counsel of the Warren estate. I was confident that the property could be purchased at a price much less than that, and which would meet the approbation of the people. By the agreement entered into yesterday between the representative of the city and of the Warren estate, the park will be purchased for $110,000. This will be the entire sum that will be paid to the Warren estate, and the only additional expense will be the payment by the city (if condemnation proceedings are decided upon as the better way to obtain title, which will be secured amicably) of the expenses of the commissioners. The Warren estate has agreed to pay its own counsel fees. As the sum has already been agreed upon by both parties, the legal procedure will be short and quickly disposed of.

"I feel that in securing possession of a public park of seventy acres in the heart of the city, with beautiful natural endowment, and with an unsurpassed view and accessible to that large population that has been shut off from the enjoyment of any park facilities, I have carried out the desires of the people of this city. I have no doubt that the future park as a place for resort, for rest, for recreation and for the improvement of mind and body which come with pure air and a large outlook, will increasingly commend itself to the pride and affection of the people of Troy, and will more and more justify the wisdom of securing this place at the most advantageous time and under the most advantageous conditions for the use of the people of this city and their descendants for generation to come."

A Landscape Architects Opinion

In connection with the purchase of the park property it is interesting to recall the opinion given by Edward Lincoln Raymond, a well known landscape architect with offices in New York, Boston, and Buffalo. In a letter written to Mayor Conway May 9 1901, Mr. Raymond gives the following as his views with regard to the Warren Hill property after a personal investigation of the place:

"I have been asked in regard to the eligibility of the Warren Hill property for the purpose of a public park. I looked carefully over the piece of land known as Warren Hill. It has many of the conditions that are desirable in choosing a site for a park, namely, accessibility, rolling topography and delightful view together with more or less of a natural growth.

The elm beetle has worked destructively on the American elms on this property; the remaining trees are soft maples, with here and there a scattered oak, together with a large assortment of fruit trees. It is general recognized that fruit trees have no place in a park, so that the fruit trees at present existing should only be allowed to remain until new forest trees planted in their midst, and sheltered by these same fruit trees acting as nurses, should attain a degree of growth as would enable them to stand alone and by of some beauty.

And an enlarged city square, accessible to a large proportion of the poor of Troy, it is an ideal spot: with a superb outlook, and outlook which I have seldom seen surpassed, containing between thirty and forty acres of level land about rolling enough to afford variety and capable of being so developed as to form a most pleasing breathing spot.

It has been sad that the foot of the hill surrounding this property will have to be bolstered up with a terrace wall. I would not say that a low wall might not be necessary, but as an engineer of quite a varied experience I would say that, in my opinion, the greater portion of this hillside has reached such an inclination will stop further landslide. I looked carefully over the soil with the gardener in care of the property, whose knowledge of the ground beneath our feet gained by actual digging in the same gave his remarks great weight, and I found sufficient to keep up this hillside and in many places are areas of gravel. If such poor

[Line missing from microfilm]

seen from many points, and which is certainly a blemish to the landscape, would be changed to a thing of beauty, and I see no reason why this could not be done. On some sides the slope is not so precipitous as to rule out paths, and they would afford delightful opportunity for rest, together with a charming prospect. The roads of the flat area of this property are to a great degree made. Very little expense would be incurred by the city for road building on this property, which is an important item. I think in a few years this Warren Hill property could be developed into one of the most charming little breathing spots that I have ever seen. The city of St. John utilizes a hill overlooking the Bay of Fundy, Montreal overlooking the St. Lawrence, New Britain, Conn overlooks its factories and the city proper, and many other cities have utilized their hills in their immediate precincts as points of observation or miniature parks.

I feel confident that if the city of Troy can purchase this property at a reasonable figures that no mistake will be made, and neither will it interfere with the development of the future park system of the city of Troy, lying to the north and south of the city. It will be only in advance of the development of parks on a liberal scale marking an enlarged breathing spot in the center, and if the city of Troy grows as we have all reason to suppose in the future with the rapidity that it has grown in the past this Warren Hill property will be surrounding on all sides with a large number of people. I suppose at present there are 10,000 people within a half a mile of it. The purchase and development of this property will be the initiative move in the development of parks for the city of Troy. In a city like Albany, a residential town whose growth has been obtained in great measure, a different state of affairs exists, but in a manufacturing town like Troy, we have very reason to suppose that the city will grow, and from the peculiar conditions existing a park will be necessary in the north and south portions, Warren Hill answering for the center."

On March 27th in the Troy Daily Times an informed citizen with the pen name CIVIS published a letter to the editor:

"The Assessed Valuation

Editor Troy Times:

The local writer of the article in your paper today, head "A New Park." with a view to approve of the purchase of the Warren Hill property said: "It is nearly $30,000 less than the assessed valuation." This writer is hereby informed that nine-tenths of the realty of this city is valued on the Assessors' books at from twenty-five per center to fifty per cent more than it will sell for an more than it is daily selling for a private sale and at auction. CIVIS.
Troy, March 26, 1902"

The city wasted no time surveying the property so it could obtain the deed:

April 8, 1902, Troy Daily Times

"City engineer Cary has begun a survey of the Warren Hill property, so that a description can be made for a deed of the property of the city. The park will soon be in the possession of the city and will at once be thrown open to the public."

"Rose in Prospect Park" by C.O.N. (1912)

Rose in Prospect Park.
BY C. O. N.

From fair Mount Ida's western slope,
I've gazed with rapture and with hope,
While 'cross the valley's wide expanse
The billowy shadows play and prance;
The noble Hudson seaward flows,
Yet I see nothing but my Rose.

Fair maidens, lithe of limb and arm,
At tennis play, with wond'rous charm;
The summer sun beams from above,
While they shout gayly "Deuce" and "Love."
Still I, on sidelines, lie and doze,
Seeing nothing but my Rose.

The children, in the sand and swings,
Like fairies seem, tho' minus wings;
Their Spring of Life is near overflowing,
They care not how the wind is blowing.
Their shouts disturb not my repose,
For I see nothing by my Rose.

She is a picture past compare,
With wide-brimm'd hat and waving hair;
Her racket poised to serve the ball,
Her graceful figure, slender, tall.
Enraptured, 'thralled, my eyes I close
And still see nothing but my Rose.

Fatigued, she seeks a shady nook,
Where, quiet, she can read her book.
Her dropping lashes kiss her cheeks,
Her voice is music when she speaks;
And when she smiled each flower let glows—
They, too, see nothing but my Rose.

Ah! would that no one else were near,
I'd gladly, fondly, call her "Dear."
Alas! our fondest hopes are vain—
Just at that moment down came rain,
And, trembling, like one partly froze,
I then see—nothing of my Rose.

Troy Times. September 3, 1912: 9 col 1.

Chapter Four
The Rise and Fall of Prospect Park

On March 26th, 1901, Troy had a new park called Warren Hill Park on top of Mount Ida. For the next few months, the details of the park plan found its way into the newspaper. It would take several years under the direction of Garnet D. Baltimore to create the park. This included making new roads and entrances to the park from all directions, building fences, creating a lake, band shell, observation tower, building playgrounds and tennis courts, and removing hundreds of fruit trees and landscaping from the more than 100 years of previous private ownership. Each year, more and more progress would be made culminating with the building a brand new above ground swimming pool in 1926. Prospect Park became the jewel of the city and thousands of Trojans enjoyed all the amenities for over fifty years. Many a Trojan played baseball, basketball, croquet, tennis, ran track and learned to swim. Thousands of younger children played with others on merry go rounds and swings. The two mansions of former days were turned into a museum called Memorial Hall (Warren Mansion) where you could learn about military history and have a snack on the porch of the Vail Mansion (Casino). The mansions even served as a temporary school when School 14 burned to the ground. Read on now as we relive the history of the building of the park and the memories of thousands who once called Prospect Park the place to learn, play, and be happy:

1902 May 19 Troy Daily Times

"Municipal Problems

Rev. Andrew Gillies speaking at State Street Methodist Church on the subject "The Modern City: Its complex problems and their solution."

"We are, it is true, planning for a breathing spot on Warren Hill, but that is but an apology for what we ought to be doing. There are a dozen spots in this city where rookeries ought to be torn down, rubbish cleared away and places of recreation for children established."

1902 June 14 Troy Daily Times

With the Fourth of July celebration on Warren Hill, the city certainly ought to have a high old time on the anniversary day of American independence. The American flag on that summit will be a conspicuous object in the landscape, and will speak for miles around of the patriotism and public spirit of this city."

The formal opening of Warren Hill Park would be the Fourth of July, 1902 a year after it was first proposed and plenty of activities were planned:

1902 July 3 Troy Daily Times

"For the 4th of July celebrations

8:00 AM – Colonel Lloyd and staff, music and companies A, C and D, Second Regiment, board chartered cars at Third and Congress Streets and proceed to Warren Hill Park.

8:30 AM – Military ceremonies at Warren Hill Park. Escort of the colors and flag rising. Review of military companies in command of Col J.B. Lloyd before Mayor Conway, city officials and prominent citizens at reviewing stand.

9 AM- Firing national salute of twenty-one guns by detachment of artillery from Watervliet arsenal, and response from guns at dock of Watervliet Arsenal.

10 AM- Band concert at stand in Warren Hill Park by Doring's Band.

BAND CONCERTS

2:30-4 PM. At Warren Hill Park by Troy Cadet Band.

Band stand at Warren Park will be built by George Spence.

Opening of the Park

The public observance of the day in this city will be largely confined to the formal opening of Warren Hill Park on the morning of July 4 and a series of band concerts given at central points throughout the city during the day. As no improvements have as yet been made to the park property the formal dedication of the park will not take place until a later date.

The day will open with the ringing of bells throughout the city.

Col. James H. Lloyd and staff and Field Music of the Second Regiment, with Companies A, C and D, will board cars at the corner of Congress and Third Streets at 8 o'clock and will proceed to the park. Carriages will be provided for Mayor Daniel E. Conway, members of the Common Council, members of the Board of Contract and Supply and Special Independence Day Committee.

Military Exercises

The military ceremonies at the park in the morning will consist of the escort of the colors, which will be unfurled from the flagpole erected in the park. The military companies, in command of Colonel Lloyd, will pass in review before the stand erected for the occasion, and on which will be stationed Mayor Conway, the city officials, members of the Independence Day Committee and a number of prominent citizens, who have been invited to participate in the ceremonies. A national salute of twenty-one guns will be fired from two cannon by a detachment of artillery from the Watervliet Arsenal, and a response will be made from guns stationed on the dock at the Watervliet Arsenal, under the direction of Colonel Farley, Commandant. The guns will be fired at intervals of thirty seconds.

At the conclusion of the military ceremonies a band concert will be given at the stand in the park by Doring's Band.

Concerts will also be given during the afternoon and evening at various points in the city.

1902 July 3 Troy Daily Times

The local celebration of the Fourth of July, with the flag raising in the new park on Warren Hill, stands for freedom. It means free air and free parks, and what boon of liberty is greater than to have the earth and the sky free? As the flag shakes out its folds to greet the starry emblem at the military post of the United States across the river, and as salute answers salute, Troja can remark to Columbia, "When it comes to liberty, I am with you."

1902 July 3 Troy Daily Times Afternoon

Tomorrow Celebration

Flag raising and review of military companies at Warren Hill Park – The band concerts at Warren Hill Park – The Band Concerts – Program of the day.

All arrangements for the celebration of Independence Day in Troy have been completed and the program promises an observance that will be greatly enjoyed. It will be particularly interesting, as it includes the formal opening to the public of Warren Park, Troy's new pleasure and recreation ground. The principal event of the day will take place in the park at 8:30 o'clock in the morning, when there will be a military ceremony of the escort to the colors and the new flag will be unfurled. The Mayor and other city officials and guests of the city will be present, and Doring's Band will render patriotic airs.

Following the raising of the colors, Mayor Conway will review the local military companies, including the Sixth Separate Company, Capt. Edward F. Roy commanding; the Twelfth Separate Company, Capt. William Baker commanding, and the Twenty-first Separate Company, Capt. William J. Galbraith commanding. Col. James H. Lloyd of the Second Regiment and staff and the non-commissioned staff will participate in the ceremonies.

Musical Features

Immediately after the ceremonies there will be a concert by Doring's Band.

The salute to the colors will be fired from two guns from the Watervliet Arsenal, manned by a detachment of United States Artillery. A response salute will be fired from the Arsenal.

Band concerts will be given in the afternoon at various places in the city by Doring's, the Troy Cadet and Abrams' Bands.

A Souvenir Program

J.H. McGrath has issued a handsome program of the events to comprise the celebration. It contains portraits of Mayor Conway, the Chairmen of various sub-committees of the General Independence Day Committee, the members of the Board of Contract and Supply, Col. James H. Lloyd and Assemblyman John F. Ahern, who introduced the bill that gave Troy a park.

The Band Concerts

Following are the programs of the band concerts to be held in the afternoon:

DORING'S

Warren Hill Park: 8:30 to 11 AM- March, "Stars and Stripes Forever," "Sousa;" overture, "America," Moses;" medley; "The World Beater," Mackie; descriptive, "Hunt in Black Forest," Volker; piccolo solo, "The Wren," "DeMare," W.F. Franke; selection, "King Dodo," Anderson; sextette from "Florodora," Stuart; intermezzo Arabian, "Gamona," Loraine; selection "Romance of Athlone," Olcott, march, "Peach Forever, " La Calel.

TROY CADET

Warren Hill Park, 2:30 to 4 PM- Grand Enter, "Caesar's Triumphal March," Mitchell; overture, "La Lac of Fees," Auber; Valse Bleue, Margis; excerpts from Meyerbeer's operas, Heinicke; piccolo solo, "The Humming Bird," DeMare, Frederic Landau; patriotic march, "The Old Veteran," Barnard; American fantasia, "Gems of Stephen Foster," Tobani; caprice "Japnonca," Stamford; medley, "Top Liners," Chattaway; march "A Frangesa," Costa.

Preparation of the Park

Commissioner of Public Works Phelan went to Warren Park this afternoon to supervise the final preparations for the ceremonies tomorrow. The raising of the colors and military review will take place on the plateau in front of the Vail residence, where there is a large cleared space. There remain a number of fruit trees to cut down, and the men were hampered in this work this morning by the rain. The flag-pole on which the new flag is to be raised is situated on a projecting point of the plateau in a southeastern direction from the residence, where the flag can be seen from all parts of the city.

Responses Received by the Mayor

Mayor Conway has received letters of acceptance to invitations to be present at the ceremonies in the park from Walter P. Warren and Gen C. Whitney Tillinghast, 2nd, President Jacob A. Cantor of the borough of Manhattan, New York; John C. Sheehan of New York and Mayor Seth Low have sent letters of regret at being unable to attend.

The following letter was received from Robert Cluett:

I am just in receipt of your invitation to attend the exercises in connection with the hoisting of the colors in the new Warren Park July 4, for which accept my thanks I need hardly say it would give me pleasure to be present, but absence from the city will prevent my attendance.

Allow me to congratulate you on the success of the efforts to provide additional parks for the city of Troy. I believe citizens in general will sustain you in carrying out such improvements and undertakings.

About fifty patrolmen detailed to Warren Park tomorrow morning to preserve order during the ceremonies. Superintendent Coughlin will be in charge of the detail."

The success of the formal opening was covered the day after:

"1902 July 5 Troy Daily Times

New Park Opened

Accidents of the Day.

Perfect weather for the city celebration – Day's events opened with the raising of the flag and the military review in Warren Hill Park – Five thousand present – Band concerts in various parts of the city – The fireworks displays.

The celebration of this city of the one hundred and twenty sixth anniversary of the Declaration of American Independence was in every way a fitting one. The day was fair and comfortably warm and those who celebrated the day with explosives and fireworks or spent the hours in enjoying some of the various forms of amusement offered found the conditions favorable.

Raising the Flag in the New Park

By far the most pleasurable feature of the day's observances in this city, and at the same time one entirely appropriate, was the raising of an American flag at Warren Hill Park to mark the formal opening of the park to the public. The exercises formed in many ways a pleasant surprise to a large majority of those present, who had not before inspected the ground and knew nothing of the natural beauties of the spot selected for Troy's first public park. On leaving the trolley cars at the Congress Street entrance to the park property the roadway leads through the trees and verdant undergrowth to a broad plateau above. There is a spacious open field surrounded on all sides by groves of stately trees, and the beauty of the scene is so striking one begins to wonder that such a refreshing spot exits in the very heart of the city.

About 5,000 Presentation

Despite the fact that the hour fixed for the exercises at the park was an early one there were fully 5,000 persons on the park grounds when Mayor Conway, heading a delegation of city officials and members of the committee in charge of the celebration, arrived at the reviewing stand at the south side of the open field just before 9 o'clock. Col James H. Lloyd and staff and members of Companies A, C and D of the Second Regiment, N.G. N.Y. headed by the Field Musicians of the regiment and Doring's Band, had arrived at the park a few minutes before, and were drawn up in battalion formation on the north side of the field, opposite the reviewing stand. The crowds of spectators lined the field on three sides, and were held back by a cordon of police in immediate command of Superintendent Coughlin and Captains Conway, McKenna, McGrath and Kirkpatrick.

Escorting the Flag.

A 9 o'clock Mayor Daniel E. Conway with Corporation Counsel Thomas S. Fagan, Commissioner of Public Works John Phelan, City Engineer E.R. Cary, Commissioner of Public Safety Mark J. Coyle, President of the Common Council Henry Schneider and Commissioner of Public Charities James E. Ryan marched to the plat which had been cleared at the brow of the hill, and directly overlooking the city from the head of Adams Street, where a seventy five foot pole had been erected. As soon as they had taken positions near the foot of the flag pole the formal ceremony of escorting the flag was conducted. The new flag, wrapped in a roll, was carried by John W. Roberts, Executive Clerk to the Mayor, and was escorted by Privates Brown and Bunce, of Company D, the state colors being carried by Sergeant Falle and the national colors by Color Sergeant Way, the whole being escorted by a detachment from Company A in command of Lieutenant Sherman. The escort was headed by Doring's Band and marched across the parade ground to the plat where the flagpole stands, and here the flag was formally delivered into the hands of the Mayor. As soon as the escort withdrew Col. Isaac F. Handy assisted in arranging and attaching the flag to the ropes, preparatory to unfurling it. As Doring's Band played "The Star Spangled Banner" the rolled flag was drawn up slowly to the top of the pole, and at the last strain Mayor Conway pulled the roped which held it, and the handsome flag swung forth to the breeze amid resounding cheers and applause that went up from the assembled throng. As the flag unfolded the first gun of the national salute pealed forth from the park grounds and was answered fifteen seconds later from the guns at the Watervliet Arsenal. The salute consisted of twenty one guns fired at intervals of thirty seconds, a detachment of artillery with two guns in command of Sergeant Hart being stationed at the park, and a similar detachment stationed on the Watervliet Arsenal dock answering the salute.

While the flag was being drawn up to place and unfurled the battalion of citizen soldiers stood at "present arms" and saluted the flag.

Passed in Review

This ceremony over, Mayor Conway and the city officials with him reviewed the local military companies. First, with the members of the regimental staff as escorts, they marched around the battalion, and then, standing at one side of the field, the command passed in review before them.

Mayor Conway and the officials then took places on the reviewing stand where were already seated Mayor Hilton of Watervliet and a number of officials of this city including Deputy

Commissioner of Public Safety Charles Corliss, Deputy Commissioner of Public Works Edmond Stanton, Fire Marshal D.J. Whalen, Civil Service Commissioner James M. Riley, city assessors Jacob V. Jacobs and Robert A. Patchke, Chairman M.F. Hemingway of the Board of Supervisors, the Common council and City clerk and the members of the special Independence Day Committee.

The battalion of military marched in review before the reviewing stand in company front formation and made a fine appearance, which called forth generous applause. The companies were out in good numbers. Rev. George Dugan of the Ninth Presbyterian Church, Champlain of Company D, was present during the ceremonies as a member of the staff of Colonel Lloyd. Company D was in command of Capt. William J. Galbraith, Company A in command of Capt. E. Frank Roy and Company C in command of Capt. William Baker. After passing before the reviewing stand the command marched to the entrance to the park, where chartered cars were boarded fro the return to the State Armory, where the members were dismissed.

One of the prominent spectators present during the flag raising exercise was Assemblyman John F. Ahern, who introduced the bill to provide for a public park in this city in the state legislature and worked earnestly toward its passage.

Band Concerts

At the conclusion of the exercises a concert was given at the park by Dorings' Band during the remainder of the morning. Another band concert was given from 3:20- to 4 o'clock by the Troy Cadet Band.

Many visited the Park

During the day large numbers of person visited the park and much favorable comment was expressed. Nothing has been done as yet toward the preparation of the park for public use beyond the removal of a few trees, and extensive improvements, which will materially add to the natural advantages of the park, will be begun at once. When the rank grass and undergrowth is removed, new roads and walks laid out, benches, seats and pavilions added and the landscape gardening completed, it is intended to conduct formal dedicatory exercises under the direction of the city officials.

A soldier overcome by the heat

While the review of the militia was in progress in the field Private O'Connor of Company C was overcome by the heat and dropped to the ground. He was carried from the field by the ambulance corps and was soon revived.

The committee's

The members of the general citizens committee on Independence Day celebration was as follows: Chairman J Thomas Dennin; Alderman John C Donnelly, W.H. Slattery, Gerald FitzGerald, Col James H. Lloyd, Con F. Burns, Michael Muldoon, Max Goodkind, John J. O'Neill, Charles H. Van Arnam, Jacob Birkmayer, and Alderman Marshall L. Barnes."

With the park finally opened to the public however came the hard part, creating improvements in the park to make it accessible and park like and paying for it all."

1902 September 19 Troy Daily Times

"The new city park on Warren Hill can now be called a city park, title having been acquired by the city and the Common Council having initiate last evening the arrangements for paying the purchase money. This park is a good investment for public health and pleasure, and the number of visitors already, before the formal acquirement of the land by the city, has been so large as to show that the place will be a popular center of resort."

1902 September 19 Troy Daily Times Afternoon

"Aside from the estimate, the matter of issuing bonds for the purchase and improvement of Warren Hill Park was brought up, as well as the issuance of bonds for over $30,000 for public improvements.

Communications were received from the Commissioner of Public Works submitting the deeds – six in number – of the property to be taken for the public park and an estimate of the moneys needed for the purchase, improvement and laying out of the park, and from the Corporation Counsel approving the deeds. The purchase price of the property is $110,000 and the cost of laying out and embellishing the park is fixed at $50,000. The resolution presented by the Board of Estimate and Apportionment for the issuance of bonds form the amount to be known as Troy City Park bonds, payable in thirty-two annual installments, beginning October 1, 1910, was referred to the Finance Committee.

Apparently there was a need to change the name of the park. Warren Park was not making the grade so the local press had a contest for a new name. As seen here in the Brooklyn Daily Eagle, quoting from the Troy paper, Prospect Park was in the lead, the Common Council liked it, and Brooklyn and Troy are very similar in appearance at the time so taking a hint from Brooklyn's Prospect Park, the name was changed. Ironic also that Brooklyn's park was designed by Charles Martin, an RPI engineering graduate.

1903 June 20 Brooklyn Daily Eagle

"Prospect Park is admirable alliterative and beautifully Brooklynish – Troy Press (Dem). This editorial paragraph was suggested by the adoption of the title Prospect Park for the new Troy *park on Warren Hill by the Troy Common Council. "The name." says the Press "is included in the large number of suggestions received by the Press in response to its invitation to the people to compete for an award to be given the one who suggested the name that would be selected."*

For the next few years the park was sculptured with winding roads, a man made lake, tennis courts, and playgrounds under the supervision of Garnet D. Baltimore, the city's landscape engineer and who also had the distinction of being the first African American graduate of Rensselaer Polytechnic Institute. He took his job seriously. Baltimore prepared annual reports to the City Council on the progress and problems of creating Prospect Park and they were covered widely in the Press. It appears that 1904 to 1909 were the years that serious improvements occurred. We can follow the progress from the paper and the annual reports:

Work being conducted in 1904.

1904 June 2 Troy Times

"The Enjoined Commissioner

Under Justice Herrick's Modified order Commissioner of Public Works is instructed to hire men for park and waterworks – report of landscape engineer Baltimore.

An important report showing the condition of the Prospect Park funds and the needs of the park was submitted at the meeting of the Municipal Improvements Commission this morning. The enjoined commission met about 10:30 o'clock, the Mayor, Corporation Counsel and commissioner of Public Works being present. The approval of the minutes was deferred.

Resolutions to Hire Men

A resolution was then adopted that Mr. Baltimore's report be received and that the Commissioner of Public Works be empowered to secure the services of men, teams, etc. to provide for the progress and care thereof, as recommended in the report of the Landscape Engineer. The Commissioner of Public Works and the Superintendent of Waterworks were authorized to secure the men necessary to operate the pumping station and to place the same in operation at once. Bills were referred to the Commissioner of Public Works.

Report of Landscape Engineering

The report of landscape Engineer Baltimore in full follows:

Landscape Engineer Office, Prospect Park, May 31, 1904

Municipal Improvements Commission.

Gentlemen: In accordance with the resolution of your honorable body adopted at the regular meeting May 27, 1904, "That the Landscape Engineer, Garnett D. Baltimore, be requested to communicate recommendations to this Commission as to the plan and scope of the embellishment, beautification, and improvement of the park areas, the estimate cost, the number of men, labor and services require: the cost of the land necessary to acquire, and other information or recommendations germane to the mater." I would respectfully report as follows:

Financial

The Comptroller's report to the Commission of May 26, 1904 shows the money appropriated and expended for Prospect Park as follows:

Sale of Park bonds, October, 1902 in pursuance of Chapter 185, laws of 1901 – Principal............$160,000.00

Premiums and interest.......$4,268.30

Miscellaneous receipts......$116.00

Total $164,382.30

Expenditures...........164,035.34

Balance on hand to audit.......$346.96

Outstanding claims: Contract to John F. Knauff & Co, $1399; a claim of the waterworks Department for the sum of $2362.33; total $3761.33 or a deficit of $3414.37

In the preliminary estimate of this year there was included for parks the sum of $17, 776, divided as follows:

Statement of expenditures in the Department of Public Parks from January 1 to May 26, 1904:

Work being conducted in 1904.

Superintendent of Parks	Appropriation	Expended	Balance
Super of parks	900	300	600
Landscape engineer	2000	622.11	1377.99
Rodman	600	115	485
Caretakers	1776	226.12	1549.88
Watchmen	4320	526.80	3793.20
Teams	2000	110	1890
Laborers	3200	349.50	2850.50
Flowers & Shrubbery	1000		
Care and improvement	2000	316.82	1683.18

From the several items of balances are to be deducted the salaries and expenses accrued during the month of May.

Recommendations

It is to be sincerely regretted that the work of improving Prospect Park has been so seriously interrupted at this, the most favorable season of the year for park work, the park, when the people should be able to enjoy its facilitates, being in a most uninviting and unattractive condition. It cannot therefore be urged too strongly upon the Commission the necessity for the immediate resumption of work under intelligent supervision. The entire Plateau of the park should be graded and turned as rapidly as possible into lawn. The play stead should be pushed rapidly to completion, so that it could be available for tennis, croquet and other games before the summer passes.

I recommend therefor for Prospect Park that the following force be organized at once, consisting of a rodman, who can also act as timekeeper: one foremen, $2.50 per day; one Gardner, $2 per day; fifteen laborers, 1.50 per day, and three teams, $5 per day; the entire force to be in direct charge and under the supervision of the Landscape Engineer. It has been the custom to detail a caretaker at each of the following parks Seminary, Powers, Lansing, and three caretakers at Beman Park. It will also be necessary to detail a man to look after the plots adjacent to the steamer and station houses when improved.

Casino Should be closed

Sunday the building which it is intended to devote to the purposes of a casino was opened as a refreshment stand. No effort was made to make the surroundings attractive or inviting. I was unable to find that any contract had been entered into or restrictions placed upon the conduct of

A closeup of the bridge over the stream that fed into the lake seen on the left. The playground stairs can be seen in the upper left back.

The lake area today. You can still see the steps to the playground in the back.

The view of the lake.

Creating the lake in 1904.

the management by the Commission.

It is an imperative obligation of those to whom the welfare of the park is intrusted that no feature be tolerated which would tend to cheapen or belittle the character of the park. I therefore recommend that this building be closed until it is properly prepared by the Commission for the purpose intended and then conducted as a strictly first class casino.

The force of watchmen now at the park consists of three, although the estimate provides for six. The force should be increased to the full number.

Under the date of February 1, 1904, I transmitted to the Commission a report containing the following outlines and estimate for the completion of Prospect Park:

"The plans contemplate a change of the contours of the entire western and southern slopes. The slopes are to be terraced, with avenues leading from the entrances on the south and west to the main plateau. It is necessary in order to obtain a suitable slope that the park area be extended to the east line of Havermans Avenue. The assessed valuation of the property is $21,050. The acquisition of this property would give a boundary of the park on a street and then the projected retaining wall could be built upon the east line of Havermans Avenue."

At present there is no means of reaching the park from the south and west where many of the people to be benefited reside.

Enlarging Park Limits

It is also contemplated to include the old Mount Ida Cemetery in the park limits, to enclose the grounds by a fence and, if nothing more, exercise care and supervision over the land: The plans conceive the building of a canal or lagoon east of the Congress Street entrance and at the rear of St Francis' Church. The canal is to be spanned by artistic bridges, a portion of the island to be created as a rose and herbaceous garden.

Additional amusement features are to be added as the development of the park progresses. The tennis and croquet grounds are to be in readiness for this season.

Estimate for Completion

Acquisitions of land $30.000
Electric lighting, conduit system 3000
masonry, retaining wall, etc. 15,000
Sewers and drains 5,000
broken stone for roads 20,000
tress and shrubbery 5,000
propagating house 3000
benches 2600
bridges 2500

swings, merry go rounds, etc. 2500
signs, cans receptacles 500
labor and teams 25,000
soil extra black 2000
materials 2000
fencing 5000
buildings painting and repairing 3000
furnishing buildings 1000
supplies 2000
driving foundations, shelters, etc. 1000
contingencies 900
Total 150,000

The estimates provides for no salaries it being assumed that the salaries would be provided in the annual estimate.

Property to be acquired

List of property to be acquired for the enlarging of the park area of Prospect Park: Lots No 79, 81, 88, west side of Chestnut Street, assess valuation 5200; about three and one half acres of the side hill, belong to Andrew Ruff; lots 5,6,7,8,9, 10 west side of Congress Street, owned by the Mann estate and Harris, assessed valuation 6060; Church lot and lot east of the cottage road, on Congress Street, William Crowley, estate owner, 300; Warren estate plot of ground bounded on the north by Kennedy & Murphy, east by Prospect Park, south by Liberty St, west by Troy Union Railroad; asses valuation 5000; lots A B 75 and 1-40, inclusive, east side of Havermans Avenue, assess valuation 21,050.

A bill embracing the amount $150,000 for the completion of Prospect Park was introduced into the last legislature and has since become a law. The necessity for the completion of the park appealed so strongly to our intelligent citizen that practically no opposition was manifested.

It now rests with the Commission to take the necessary steps and urge upon the proper authorities the necessity of making the amount appropriate available for the completion of the work, so that Prospect Park may not only become an object of pride but a spot where our citizens may enjoy recreation and the beauties of nature with an appropriate environment.

Respectful submitted

Garnett D. Baltimore"

Much work was organized and completed during 1905. With the help of the city's Women's League (Women's Improvement Society), and in particular Mrs. Frank W. Thomas, part of the park was converted to playgrounds in 1906 in the area behind the Vail House. The playground

The construction of the fountain area and flower beds in 1904.

was opened in June to much fanfare. This included a cast iron drinking fountain donated by Mrs. Ellen Bascom in memory of her husband.

The playground movement in the United States began around 1880 for children and over two decades expanded to all ages. Troy, admittedly by its own residents was a bit slow to get on the bandwagon but credit must be given to the Woman's League for getting if off the ground and on the ground at Prospect Park. Although it was not until 1890 that the real push toward park provisions were seen in municipalities. In 1852 there was not a single municipal park in America. By 1892, 100 cities had parks. By 1926, 250,000 acres had been set aside by about 1,680 cities. In 1905 the Playground and Recreation Association of America was formed.

This was also a psychological shift as to the purpose of parks which went from *"a place where urban inhabitants could obtain the recreation coming from the peaceful enjoyment of its rural, sylvan, and natural scenery and character,"* to a wide range of active forms of recreation like tennis, croquet, athletics, and swimming. There was also the belief that parks were just plain "healthy" for you. As one writer asserted: *"Recreation is of value not only in preserving the health of the individuals, but also in the treatment of physical and mental ailments."*

This also created the need for new park administrations and specialized labor to deal with the complexities of running the park. By 1928 some 176 cities in the United States, representing

The erection of rustic fences in 1904.

one fifth of the total population, had general plans including comprehensive park plans and 390 cities had implemented planning boards to direct development along these lines.

1906 Troy Times April 28

"The plans of the Woman's League have been now so shaped that soon a considerable section of Prospect Park will begin to assume the appearance of summer recreation grounds for children. Mayor Mann, who has shown great interest in the project, has through the President of the league. Mrs. Frank W. Thomas granted for this purpose the section within a radius of 250 feet above the old Vail residence; also a part of the Vail house to be fitted up for kindergarten work on rainy days, when the children cannot enjoy the grounds themselves.

This part of the park is peculiarly fitted for the purpose, as it is well shaded – a condition not always found on public playgrounds, but very essential to the comfort and welfare of the children during the hot months. Prospect Park, with lofty situation, its commanding view and invigorating breezes, is an inviting summer resort; and while the beauty of the outlook may not appeal to the young people, the fine air they will breathe for a large part of the day cannot fail to give much physical benefit."

1907 June 23 Troy Daily Times

The Women's Improvement League

Mrs. Kenney read the announcement of the opening of the playground at Prospect Park. The playground will be opened Thursday afternoon at 2 o'clock. There will be music during the afternoon by Doring's Orchestra, and Fred C. Comstock, baritone, will contribute several vocal solos to the program. The playground apparatus will be in readiness for the use of the children, under the direction of the kindergarten teachers who direct the play, Miss Reynolds, Miss Comiskey, and Miss Persch. The kindergarten rooms will be open for public inspection and the governing Board of the Woman's Improvement League will hold an informal reception on the piazza of the Vail House.

1907 Annual Report Vol 8 Troy Public Improvement Commission

"Most substantial evidence of public spirit and civic pride, however, came through the generosity of Mrs. Ellen F. Bascom in tendering to the park the H. Clay Bascom Memorial drinking fountain, which will prove not only a source of refreshment to the thousands who visit the park, but will keep forever fresh."

"Henry Clay Bascom was the owner of the Vedder Pattern Works (1884) working his way up from accountant for the company. He was a well known Prohibitionist and was a delegate to the National Prohibition conventions of 1884 and 1888, and for several years represented New York on the National Prohibition Committee. In 1883 he was the Prohibition candidate for Senator and in 1885 he was the Prohibition candidate for Governor of New York. He was also a prospective Prohibition candidate for President. An outspoken champion of reform and forceful vigorous author of articles in the press throughout the country. He was the author of Requited; or A Knight in Livery, an epic poem. He was superintendent of that department of Grace Methodist Episcopal Church in Troy and held a preaching license from there. Ellen Lucina Forbes was his second wife and also devoted much time to furthering the cause of temperance. She was a member of the Woman's Christian Temperance Union of Lansingburg, New York, having been president (1910) twenty-three years. Henry Bascom died in Florida on December 22, 1896."

The cast iron drinking fountain had provisions for both man and animal. On one side there was a horse trough, three feet nine inches by two feet and three inches and eleven inches deep. The place for people included *"two faucets, one on each side where the water flow was controlled by self closing valves operated by pushing metal buttons."* Troughs for dogs *"were filled from the overflow from the faucets."* There was a patented water cooling machine underground in the rear of the fountain where water passed through a series of coils and reservoirs encased in ice. The fountain was fifteen feet and three inches in height, with a base four feet and seven inches square. The shaft was square in section tapering in graceful lines to the top, with side brackets for electric lights. On the front was *"H. Clay Bascom Memorial Fountain. Presented to the City of Troy by Ellen F. Bascom, 1907. The draped figure of Hebe from the original statue of the artist Thorwaldsen will surmount the ornamental capital. The figure was five feet in height and stood in graceful attitude, with a vessel of water extended in one hand and the other hand holding a pitcher at her side."* It was located just south of the Warren mansion on the west side of Prospect Avenue (the former name for the present main road) near its intersection with Sylvan Avenue (I believe that is the old Vail's Road). The location was located so that *"practically all that visit the park will pass and be visible from all points of the main plateau."* It was *"in the midst of noble trees and its artistic lines will add much to the appearance of Troy's beautiful park."* It was common for water fountains to serve both humans and animals. There is a good example of one at the corner of Beman Park at 15th Street and People's Avenue. The question now is what happened to the drinking fountain?

1907 October 24 Troy Daily Times

The Progress of Prospect Park

A very interesting statement, showing in detail what money has been expended and what work has been accomplish in the improvement of Prospect Park since January 1, 1906, had been submitted to Commissioner of Public Works Schneider by Landscape Engineer Garnet D. Baltimore. It outlines the numerous improvements made during the last two summers, and the wonderful progress toward the completion of the park, which is patent to all who have visited the city's beautiful park recent. While the accomplishments have been so much greater than ever before, the work has been performed by a greatly reduced number of employees through larger efficiency. During the last summer the maximum force has been thirty-four men, thee teams and one single horse, and in 1906 it was fifty three men and four teams, as compared with 142 men and twelve teams in 1905. Although the force this season has been comparatively small the standard of maintenance has been kept up along with the steady progress of the improvements. The statement of the cost of Prospect Park shows that the total actual cost for the purchase of land, improvement and maintenance to October 15 was $156,738.44 of which $110,000 was paid for the property. During the present year, although Troy has a comparatively new park and the improvement cost would naturally be great the report shows that Troy will expend only a little more than one third of what Albany will expend upon it park system. The report commends the public spirit and civic interest which inspired the presentation of the H. Clay Bascom Memorial Drinking Foundation, and states that at the present time a proposition from a prominent citizen to add a magnificent gift to its attractiveness is under consideration. The maintenance of the present high standard of attractiveness and beauty is urged, and the report also suggests the provision of athletic fields and playgrounds in various parts of the city,

The annual reports by the Public Works Department and Baltimore for the next two years gives us a good understanding of the improvements made, the cost, and the problems experienced in finally getting the park finished.

1908 Dept. of Public Works annual report

Area city of Troy, 5,964.4 acres or 9.32 square miles

Lists Prospect Park at 84 acres

Power Park 2.14

Beman Park 6.28

Lansingburgh Park 2.41

Seminary Park .41

Watchman at prospect park paid $3600.

Sale of restaurant privilege prospect park $180.

Progress in the development of Prospect Park has been substantial and altogether satisfactory and the various accomplishments noted.

The beautiful Bascom memorial foundation, gratefully acknowledge in the last report of this bureau, was erected and throughout the season dispensed its refreshing waters to the frequenters of the park.

Two historic cannon, relics of the Civil War were placed on solid concreted foundations near the flag staff, with dedicatory exercises on Memorial Day.

One of the greatest necessities was provided on the evening of the 18 of June, when the electric lighting system was placed in operation.

It is urgent recommend that four additional lamps be authorized, to be situated in situations where illumination is obvious required and that two lamps be early installed to light the new approach from Jefferson Street.

Tennis grounds were appreciably amplified by the opening of four new courts which afforded opportunity for enjoyment of this popular and healthful pastime to a greater number of devotees of the sport. For the convenience of players occupying the courts, a shelter should be erected on the edge of the field, having been a noticeable lack in time past.

On the children's playground the little ones in daily attendance to the average of 500, thoroughly enjoyed the devices with which this reserve is equipped. With commendable zeal the Woman's Improvement League of Troy has brought about the establishment of another playground in the North End and ....?

The Sunday band concerts during the summer regularly attracted appreciative auditors and furnished entertainments always enjoyable to assemblages of people numbering upwards of 5,000 on the respective occasion.

The boys athletic field has been graded and will be seeded at as early a date as feasible, to evolve a conditions insuring much usefulness in serving the purpose of its inception a site more extensive in area, which with some grading and filling would accommodate contests of older athletes, is comprised in the natural enclosure on the southern slope of the park, along the curvature of the new avenue, and might well be developed for outdoor games.

The band stand has been painted and equipped with new canvas awnings, likewise the Casino Porch.

The roofs of the memorial Hall and the Casino have received necessary repairs, including painting; and new water and gas piping connections have been made in the Memorial Hall, the last mentioned work having an artistic culmination in the erections, over the outer balcony of the Hall, of a memorial lamp donation by the Tibbits Veteran Corps of Troy, and which originally adorned the main entrance to the Centennial Exhibition of 1876. The military museum with its interesting exhibits is attracting large numbers of visitors. Contributions of pictures, emblems and curios are invited from citizens and are acceptable at all times.

The Casino building and the porches and woodwork of the Memorial Hall should be painted, as it is quite some time since this has been done, especially in the case of the first named structure.

The location of the men's lavatory should be at once changed from the Casino, where it is too close proximity to the kindergartener and the ladies retiring room. Several places, much less objectionable, are available in remote quarters.

The roads and footpaths through the park were resurfaced with a layer of stone screenings and a number of dead trees were removed, each performances making for improvement of the grounds in condition and appearance.

THE GIRL WITH THE CUP residing in Prospect Park, above, looks down over midtown Troy. The statue adorns a memorial to Henry Clay Bascom erected in 1908.

The girl with the cup residing in Prospect Park looks down over midtown Troy. The statue adorns a memorial to Henry Clay Bascom erected in 1908. Where did it go?

The Band Shell above and the overlook shelter on the south east side of the park in 1904.

Trees sprayed for infections.

Residents of the southern community will in the future be enabled to gain access to the park more readily and with less physical exertion than has been heretofore exacted. The new roadway from Jefferson Street is in an advanced stage of construction and with the opening of the coming season will be rapidly brought to completion.

On a number of occasion during the year Prospect Park was the scene of public exercises, conducted by various civic organizations, patriotic societies, military bodies and public school assemblages.

In May the school children celebrated Arbor Day planning trees with attendant appropriate ceremonies.

On Memorial day, at the ceremonies attending the mounting of the cannon, as mentioned, prominent veterans of the Civil and Spanish wars delivered addresses, response being made by his Honor, the Mayor and the Tibbits Cadets of this city, Co D, 2nd Regiment USNY with its old guard, extended the customary line of march of its annual parade and took park in the exercise.

In September last our citizens observed "Old Home Week" and the parks were inspected during that time by admiring throngs include thousands of visitors from various sections. Prospect Park was the scene of a number of gatherings arranged in the program of that memorably successful celebration and again was demonstrated the appropriateness of the place for the accommodation of such functions as were conducted there from the opening to the closing of the celebration.

The most elaborate and inspiring spectacle of the exercises in the park was afforded by the observance of "Church Day" which was marked by an ably conducted parade of Sunday School children, who were led in graceful order and disposed about the central stand from which they were address by the Governor and prominent state officers. The Mayor presided, a band of music rendered pleasing selections and the children under their director sang patriotic songs.

Spectators in attendance enthusiastically declared it to have been one the of the most beautiful and affective sights possible to be witnessed, as the pupils, massed in a compact body, carrying miniature American flags, lifted up their voices in song to their God and their Country.

Most of the buildings you see at the base of the mount are gone. You can see in the middle of the photo the Troy Public Library and to the right of it the County Court House.

It is pleasing to note, furthermore, the perfect order maintained and freedom from serious accidents enjoyed throughout the proceedings, which held the attention of an audiences of fully 30,000 people.

Respectfully submitted

Wm H. Cahill, Supt of Parks

Report of the Landscape Engineer, Garnet Baltimore

As has been the case since the inception, Feb 27, 1903, of the work of laying out, improving and embellishing Prospect Park, and in conformity with the agreement entered into Feb 19, 1903, in which the duties of the Landscape Engineer were defined "That as such engineer he shall cause all necessary grades to be established,

The observation tower in 1904. Location is where the TROY stones are today.

make the necessary maps, designs and profiles for the establishment and improvement of said park and its approaches, and perform all other necessary landscape engineering in and about said park and its approaches, and superintend the execution of the said plans and works." The entire design and creation of the work has been the exclusive function of the Landscape Engineer, while the merely perfunctory duties of protecting the property and maintain order have been to other hands.

It seems eminently fitting in a public work which so vitally affects the interests of the people as a public park that an accounting of its stewardship should be annually rendered. There are some good citizens, lacking in public spirit, who are prone to condemn any expenditure for civic improvement. Modern municipalities, however, have long since awakened to the fact that in striving to create the city beautiful its reflection would be caught in the beauty of the lives of its citizens. What is cost in dollars when measured by the heights to which good citizenship can attain?

Parks are the strongest factors for the upbuilding of the masses; their influence reaches up into the home of wealth and bids the inmates share its beauty. It stoops gently over the cradle in the home of poverty and sustains the wearied mother while she brings her babe into its healthful air and invigorating shade. Thus, ever drawing us back to nature, it makes possible community with the infinite.

A citizen, who standing in the presence of the great throng which assembled to open the exercises of Old Home Week and welcome the chief executive of our state, and who saw that magnificent spectacle, enhanced by the setting of the park, of thousands of children marching beneath the flag and in their evolutions noted class, creed and conditions blend and met into the folds of the Stars and Stripes, was no proud of his city and its park, sadly lacks the true Trojan spirit.

The original act under which the park site was purchased, known as chapter 185 of 1901, provided for the expenditure of $160,000. Chapter 350 was of 1905, provided for $160,000; Chapter 473 was of 1906, provided for $150,000. The bond issue, 1908, was for $30,000, making the total of $340,000. The expenditures have been: Purchase of land, $110,000; additional lands, $50,000, improvements, $176,837.27.

Chapter 350 was of 1905, provided for the purchase of abutting property, so as to control and regulate the approaches to the park, thus carrying out the original plans and doing away so far as possible, with unsightly backyards and outbuildings. The natural boundaries of a park are street lines, and it should be the policy of the city to gradually acquire land with the object in view.

On July 16, 1908 approved to build the Jefferson street approach to the park.

Prospect Lake

"Graceful in contour, natural in environment, realistic in conception; with its life and movement, light and shade, the eye never wearies."

Last season the difficulty in retaining the water made it appear that there was a serious leak. In the bottom nearly two acres in extent it was somewhat of a problem to locate a leak. It was filled several times and daily scanned to determine the precise location of the weak spot.

Problem was a stone drain, they removed it, cemented the hole and that did it.

Electric lighting systems of the park was now 4500 lineal feet of subway ducts and cables, 19 concrete manhole, ten ornamental posts for lamps, with two side lights on the Bascom fountain. Cost $4974.24. Season use of electricity from Jul. 2 to Dec 4 was $419.86

Western and southern slope

The development of the elevated Plataea of the park, being well advanced, attention is drawn to the treatment of the southern and western slopes. The problem of access on the southern slope has been solved in the Jefferson Street approach. On the western slope, plans contemplate avenues leading from Liberty Street and Seventh Street to the elevated section of the park. The tentative paper location has been made and outlined. Southern approach was Jefferson street, done. The general scheme of treatment proposed is lawn and plantation effect; aiming to secure not only a pleasing foreground from the park, but forming an attractive picture for the entire center of the city.

The most unsightly portions of the western slope are the exposed clay, sand and gravel banks near the southern end. There has been a noticeable encroachment of the property owners along Havermans Avenue. After establishing the true lines, these hills should be graded and planted. The essential fertilizing constituents of soils are nitrogen, phosphoric acid and potash. It is only necessary to supply the plant food constituent lacking through the use of the proper fertilizer to cover these unsightly hills with verdure.

1909 February 20 Letter

"Landscape Engineer Garnet D. Baltimore has received a letter from Mrs. Sarah A. Kenney in regard to his suggestion for the improvement of the city by acquiring the property on the edge of Prospect Park to enlarge the park. Mr. Baltimore has always had an ambition to secure the land, and in his report this year to the Commissioner of Public Works he urged it. Mrs. Kenney's letter follows:

"Feb. 17, 1909.

My Dear Mr. Baltimore:

I was delighted with that part of your annual report on the park system of our city which referred to the transformation of Congress Street by making that portion of it 'between the rocks' into a parkway and a fitting entrance to Troy's most attractive residence district. Ever since I came to live on the hill I have had a vision of what might be done with those rocks, so ugly and vulgar now, but to the eye of the landscape artist so capable of being transformed into things of beauty and delight. In imagination I could see them clothed with a drapery of vines, gorgeous in their autumn tints. I could see waving fern-plumes and the exquisite wildflowers which love the rock environment, all making a veritable nature garden for children's children to study and enjoy, and I have ached to be rich enough to add such a bit of loveliness to the resources of our not too beautiful city. What an object lesson for all time such a spot in the heart of our home town would be! Perhaps in the sweet bye and bye—the Golden Age which is surely to come—such a consummation will materialize. Just now the vision tarries; but what a magnificent opportunity for somebody!

For beauty achieved and dreamed, I am

Cordially yours,

SARAH A. KENNEY.

6 Larch Avenue, East Side.

"Gateway to the East Side." Troy Times. February 20, 1909."

1909 Feb 16 Troy Times

"The Report of Parks

Interesting Document submitted to the Commissioner of Public Works – History of the growth of Prospect Park – Financial Statement – Important Recommendations.

Landscape Engineer Garnet D. Baltimore this afternoon submitted his annual report to Commissioner of Public Works Shields. The report deals with the history of the growth of the park system of this city and with its financial condition and certain important recommendations are made. The report in part follows:

Troy, NY February 1909

Hon William H. Shields, Commissioner of Public Works

Dear Sir: In accordance with the established custom of the department, I have the honor to submit the following report:

As has been the case since the inception February 27, 1903, of the work of laying out, improving and embellishing Prospect Park and in conformity with the agreement entered into February 19, 1903, in which the duties of the Landscape Engineer were defined, "That as such engineer he shall cause all necessary grades to be established, make the necessary maps, designs and profiles for the embellishment and improvement of said park and its approaches, and perform all other necessary landscape engineering in and about said park and its approaches and superintend the execution of the said plans and work." The entire design and creation of the work has been the exclusive function of the Landscape Engineer, while e the merely perfunctory duties of protecting the property and maintain order have been left to other hands.

The methods of procedure under the present administration has been for the reports, recommendations and designs of the Landscape Engineer to be submitted through the Commissioner of Public Works and Board of Contract and Supply to the Mayor for approval or modification. The present stage of development of the park is, in large measure, the result of the conscientious and active supervision to the work by Mayor Mann.

The cost of Prospect Park

It seems eminently fitting in a public work which so vitally affects the interest of the people as a public park that an accounting of its stewardship should be annually rendered. There are some good citizens, lacking in public spirit, who are prone to condemn any expenditure for civic improvement. Modern municipalities, however, have long since awakened to the fact that in striving to create the city beautiful its reflection would be caught in the beauty of the lives of its citizens .What is cost in dollars when measured by the heights to which good citizenship can attain?

Parks are the strongest factors for the upbuilding of the masses; their influence reaches up into the home of wealth and bids the inmates share its beauty. It stoops gently over the cradle in the home of poverty and sustains the wearied mother while she baths her babe into its healthful air and invigorating shade. Thus, ever drawing us back to nature it makes possible communion with the infinite.

A citizen who, standing in the presence of the great throng which assembled to open the excises of Old Home Week and welcome the chief Executive of our state, and who saw that magnificent spectacle, enhanced by the setting of the park, of thousands of children marching beneath the flag and in their eveotions noted class, creed, and condition blend and melt into the folds of the Stars and Stripes, was not proud of his city and its park, sadly lacks the true Trojan spirit.

The original act under which the park site was purchased, knows as chapter 185 of 1901 , provided for the expenditure of $160,000. Chapter 350, laws of 1905, provided for $160,000; Chapter 473, laws of 1906, provided for $150,000. The bond issue, 1908, was for $30,000, making a total of $340,000. The expenditures have been: P{purchase of land, $110,000; additional lands, $50,000, improvements $176,837.27

Chapter 350, laws of 1905, provided for the purchase of abutting property so as to control and regulate the approaches to the park, thus carrying out the original plans and doing away, so far as possible, with unsightly backyard and outbuildings. The natural boundaries of a park are street lines, and it should e the policy of the city to gradually acquire land with this object in view.

The Jefferson Street Approach

From the beginning of he scheme of the development of Prospect Park the necessity of an approach from the southern section of the city was apparent. Examinations and surveys were made under the direction of the Landscape Engineer during 1903, a tentative plan was adopted and a large amount of grading and filling finished. Under the present administration the policy has been to bring to completion as rapidly as possible the elevated sections of the park, reserving the approaches for a future time. During the early part of the present season, however, this matter had been under advisement and action determined upon. At a meeting of the Common Council July 16, 1908, a resolution was introduced by Alderman Watson, inspired by the Federation Labor, providing for the approaches to the park. The resolution wend to the Public Works Committee and the matter was thus brought to the attention of Mayor Mann, who directed the Landscape Engineer to examine and report to the Board of Contract and Supply on the necessary recommendations for proceeding with the work. This he did and the work was begun August 20, 1908, On January 5, 1909, he made a report of the condition of the approach and certain recommendations. During a portion of January a small force of men were employed in the manufacture of the cement curb and gutter.

The men had attained skill and were turning out a finished product when, upon the direction of the Commissioner of Public Works, the work in the park was closed for the season.

The cost of furnishing and laying the drains, building inlets, et of the approach was as follows

21 inlet covers at $7.40 each.... $155.40

2,333 lineal feet of vitrified pipe, 15 inch, 12 inch, 10 inch, 8 inch....572.70

Cement.......100.00

Crushed stone...... 30.00

Mason on manhole.....25.00

Labor excavating and back filling, 10 men at $1.50 a day, 40 days... 600

Total $1,483.10

There had been produced up to the cessation of work, of the 4500 feet required for the preservation of this roadway, about 1200 lineal feet of the combined concrete curb and gutter. Aside from the work performed by the construction force of the park, a number of loads of materiel from without the confines of the park were delivered by city contractors. This new *approach though the park affords many opportunities for special treatment and ornamentation, while it makes accessible additional territory which enhances the entire southern slope.*

Prospect Lake

The lake since it has been in operation is one of the most attractive features of the park. Graceful in contour, natural in environment, realistic in conception, with its life and movement, light and shade, the eye never wearies. Last season the difficult of retaining the water made it apparent that there was a serious leak. In a bottom nearly two acres in extent it was somewhat of a problem to locate a leak,. The lake was therefore filled several times and daily scanned to determine the precise location of the weak spot. At length the particular place was determined, the water was drawn off and investigation disclosed several feet below the bottom of the lake a stone drain leading from the lake. This drain was removed, its place filled with concrete and thoroughly puddled and no further trouble is anticipated. A portion of the bank were sodded during the season. To complete the treatment of the lake additional planting is proposed.

Electric Lighting Systematic

The electric lighting system of the park as now constituted consists of 4500 lineal feet of subway ducts and cables, nineteen concrete manholes, ten ornamental posts for lamps, with two side lights on the Bascom fountain. The entire cost of the work, including the labor of trenching and laying ducts , was as follows:

J.L Mott iron Company, ten Edison poles at $76 each $700

M.L., Barnes conduit cables 2415.90

(M.L) Barnes wiring Bascom foundation 33.40

Mason work 15.00

Troy Gas company, writing , splicing cables, etc. 286.83

Max Grimm, tile pipe conduits 721.55

Mahoney Manufacturing Company, manhole covers 66.50

Corliss Construction Company crushed stone 125

Total 4974.24

Labor on trenches and drawing cables, etc. 1000

Total 59784.24

The entire installation with the exception of wiring the lamps and splicing the cables, was done by the employee of the park. The fact that not the slightest trouble has been experienced with the system since it was put in operation, June 18, 1908, is evidence of the thoroughness with which the work was done. The monthly cost of electric light in the park was as follows, from June 18 to Dec 1, 1908:

July 2 - 27.04

Aug 4 - 71.68

Sept 2 - 73.84

Oct 5 -78

Nov 6 - 80.60

Dec 4 - 78

Total 409.16

Bascom Fountain 10.70

Total 419.86

Additional lights will be required on the Jefferson Street approach and on the western slope as they are developed.

Western and Southern Slope

The development of the elevated Plataea of the park, being well advanced, attention is drawn to the treatment of the southern and western slopes. The problem of access on the southern slope has been solved in the Jefferson Street approach. On the western slope, plans contemplate avenues leading from Liberty Street and Seventh Street to the elevated section of the park. The tentative paper location has been made and outlined. Southern approach was Jefferson street, done. The general scheme of treatment proposed is lawn and plantation effect; aiming to secure not only a pleasing foreground from the park, but forming an attractive picture for the entire center of the city.

The most unsightly portions of the western slope are the exposed clay, sand and gravel banks near the southern end. There has been a noticeable encroachment of the property owners along Havermans Avenue. After establishing the true lines, these hills should be graded and planted. The essential fertilizing constituents of soils are nitrogen, phosphoric acid and potash. It is only necessary to supply the plant food constituent lacking through the use of the proper fertilizer to cover these unsightly hills with verdure.

1909 March 13, Troy Times

"Concerning the parks, particularly Prospect Park, the Commissioner stated that the usual time for putting full gangs of men to work had been April 15; it all depended upon the weather. The laborers were put to work when the grass began to grow. He said that the gardeners would be put at work, probably next week, in the various parks in the city, trimming shrubs and trees.

The commissioner though that the full force of men doing contract work, such as the opening of the Jefferson Street approach to Prospect Park, would not be put on until May 1. Landscape Engineer Garnet D. Baltimore this morning had a conference with the Commissioner in reference to this matter."

1910 Jan 25 Annual Report

PROSPECT PARK IMPROVEMENTS

What Has Been Accomplished in the Last Year

Reviewed in Landscape Engineers Report—Facilities For Winter Sports

Urged—For the Benefit of the People. The annual report of Landscape

Engineer Garnet D. Baltimore was submitted Thursday to the Commissioner of Public Works. The report follows:

Troy, N.Y., Jan. 25, 1910, Hon. William H. Shields, Commissioner of Public Works Dear Sir: In accordance with the annual custom of the Bureau of Parks, I have the honor to submit the following report: Introduction. In Governor Hughes' able address at the close of the Hudson-Fulton celebration were these prophetic words: "I hope that here, in Troy, by virtue of the just cooperation of the powers of nation, state and city, you may have a largely increased, as you deserve, industrial development. You have only begun in Troy to realize the advantages of your situation. You have industry and commerce; what is better, you have the civic disposition to make the best of all, and that co-operation which is the finest illustration of civic pride." The new Troy is destined to be a great industrial center. We should not plan for to-day, but for the future, not for the favored few of our citizens, but for the great mass toiling in the hives of industry. Every progressive city provides a generous supply of good and wholesome water, well paved, well lighted and clean streets, modern sanitation, good schools and places of worship. But the citizen of to-day demands and is entitled to even more than this. He looks not only into the school, but at its surroundings; not only at the public buildings, but their environment. He insists upon public places of recreation for his family and children. The city which is progressive in the true sense provides through its parks, boulevards and playgrounds that communion with nature which makes the laborer, no matter how humble, content to linger in our midst. If, then, our city is to grow industrially we must not in our development lose sight of the importance of the aesthetic features. Troy has been referred to as a beautiful city. Let us not only make it so in name but in reality. Nature has been lavish in her gifts; the streams flowing from hills on the east have furrowed cataracts, lakes and ravines that are more picturesque.

Wherever nature has been left untouched or restored beauty is triumphant. Through its parks, then, must the municipality educate and elevate its citizens to a knowledge and appreciation of nature. So that "to him who in the love of nature holds communion with her visible forms she will indeed speak a various language." Prospect Park. If Troy is fortunate in situation, Prospect Park is doubly so in location. Elevated, slightly and impressive, its summit commands a panorama of civic and natural beauty rarely equaled or excelled. Its development for the last four years has been upon judicious and economic lines; each season has seen marked improvement, bearing the record of accomplishment. The building of a park is not the creation of a day. It is the work of years, requiring all the tenderness and care which a sympathetic, loving parent gives its offspring. its results are seen in the faces of the happy throngs who frequent its sylvan precincts. The work this season, which was under the supervision of the Landscape Engineer, aside from the maintenance, consisted in grading the athletic field, the construction of, a regulation earth diamond and the building of a sixteen-foot running track, six laps to the mile. On April 27, 1909, when the field was opened, Mayor Mann formally turned it over to the President of the Public Schools Athletic League, with the understanding that the rules governing the field should give priority in use to the games of the league.

Prospect Lake.—The scenic effect of water in park treatment has always been advocated by the leading authorities, and no expense spared to secure it. Our lake, although small, is decidedly picturesque and attractive. Some trouble has been experienced in maintaining the water to its required level, owing to leakage, but this will continue to be so until a stop is put to the ignorance which persists in drawing the water down in the lake every winter, thus exposing the banks to the alternate thawing and freezing of the elements.

The Avenues.—The avenues and paths of the park have been kept up to their standard of excellence, with a light dressing of broken stone shingle. Those portions of the avenues on the side hill suffer from the erosive effect of water, and can only be properly maintained when the combined concrete curb and gutter are laid.

Trees and Shrubbery.—The trees and shrubs in the park showed the effect of judicious spring pruning, exciting favorable comment. The rose garden during June was most attractive. Judicious spraying resulted in freedom from insect pests. The elms were sprayed by contract during the season and kept free from the aphid or beetle.

The Floral Display.—The floral display was inaugurated early by a fine exhibition of tulips. Later the peonies were gorgeous in color and effect. The beds were then planted with cannas and geraniums, edged with alternanthera, Madame Celeroi and sweet alyssum. On the whole the results secured this year were successful. The beds and lawns of the Broadway approach, the reservation at the intersection of Pine Woods and Pawling Avenues and the grounds about School 14 were cared for and improved. It is to be regretted that the generosity of a public–

spirited citizen, who donated bulbs for the adornment of the High School lawns, should be marred by utter lack of harmony and the incongruity of design of the beds adopted for that purpose.

The Natural Spring.—A fine spring has for years been gushing forth on the western slope of the park. This season a water ram was purchased from The Niagara Hydraulic Engine Company and the necessary fittings from The Aird-Don Company. A concrete well house and a concrete chamber for the installation of the engine were constructed. When the engine is in operation the water will be elevated to a neat drinking fountain on the plateau of the park and the overflow returned to the bottom of the hill, where the people of the vicinity will have access to it. Owing to the lateness of the season the installation was deferred until next year.

The Tennis Courts.—The tennis courts were resurfaced this year. The popularity of tennis seems steadily on the increase. The playground was the center of attraction for the young people of all ages. The band concerts, despite counter attractions, were well attended, while the concert given by the Tenth United States Cavalry Band at the close of the Hudson-Fulton Celebration was listened to by upward of 10,000 persons.

Winter Sports in the Park. Prospect Park has the unenviable distinction of being the only park in a city of any size in this country which closes its doors to the people during winter months. It has always seemed to me that the people were entitled to its use at all seasons of the year. Prospect Lake would afford enjoyment to thousands through the most healthful of out-of-door exercise. But, the fact is, everything is done to prevent skating. When the water of the lake is at its proper level there is a surface of several acres. With the water drawn off there remains nothing but a mud puddle. One need go no further than Albany for an illustration of the advantages and pleasures of skating on a park lake. The lake should be kept full and the ice in condition for skating. There are also fine locations for toboggan slides and skiing and snowshoeing could be indulged in. Carnivals should be held, an ice palace built and efforts made to grant the people their rights to the use of the park at all seasons of the year.

The Jefferson Street Approach—The larger part of the work of construction was devoted to this approach, as a result of which there has been built an avenue following the contour of the side hill, with graceful curves and easy gradients, from the base to the summit. The permanency of its construction is evidence by the fact that there has been no appreciable settlement or washout through its entire length. The land bordering the avenue has been graded and some portions seeded. There are many attractive features susceptible to treatment which will render this portion of the park inviting. One thousand eight hundred feet of the combined concrete curb and gutter have been laid; 900(?) feet of gutter finished and stoned at the green house. The side hill location of this avenue requires for its preservation, the combined curb and gutter laid its entire length, which is 6,000(?) feet. Threes and shrubs should be planted to relieve the barrenness of the hillside a rustic fence, of a similar design to that already built, should be placed along the avenue. At the turns four electric lights are required to properly light it. A large amount of grading remains to be done in this section of the park, so as to secure the best effect. An auxiliary tennis court could be constructed on what was formerly known as the south athletic field and thus relieve the congestion of the main court.

The Western Slope.—Entrances have been established at the northern and southern sides of the park. Nothing, however, has been done to the western slope. This portion of the park is sadly in need of treatment, as it is the most conspicuous. Tentative plans have been prepared and await only the necessary funds for their execution. The park development should continue, with a moderate yearly amount for construction, separate from that of maintenance. The purchase of adjacent lands has been yearly recommended in my report, but the time has not seemed ripe for its accomplishment. The half-hearted treatment given to old Mount Ida Cemetery is not in harmony with a progressive municipality, especially after so noble an example of public spirit which the generosity of Mrs. Russell Sage afforded in Mount Ida Cemetery. There is a pleasure connected with a work of this character, which springs from the commendation and interest of citizens. A large measure of the popularity of our able executive, Mayor Mann, is due to his having given to the people of Troy Prospect Park, which appeals to their civic pride and love of nature.

Respectfully yours, GARNET D. BALTIMORE Landscape Engineer.

"Prospect Park Improvements; What Has Been

Accomplished in the Last Year Reviewed in Landscape Engineers

Report—Facilities For Winter Sports Urged—For the Benefit of the

People." Semi-Weekly Times. January 28, 1910: 8 cols 2-3.

The Park began to become a regular attraction to Troy residents and many activities such as concerts, sports events, plays, anniversary and holiday events. These events drew thousands of Trojans to the park and the city began collecting data on attendance of all parks each week with Prospect Park often having the most visitors. The Vail and Warren Mansion even served as a temporary School 14 after the old one burned and a new one was being built.

1911 Nov 17 Troy Times

The Commissioner of Public Works authorized to expend about $125 for plumbing in the old Vail House Prospect Park.

1912 March 13 Troy Times

The privileges of the Prospect Park Casino for two years were today sold to G. Konyomagian for $325 a year. This is an increase of $145 a year over the amount paid by John F. Touhey the last two years.

1919 Troy Times December 17

Oldtime Yuletime

School, 14 to revive customs on old estate

Discovery of a volume on Christmas customs prepared by the late Nathan B. Warren leads to unique program to be presented by pupils in Prospect Park – To review the pageant given on the same site more than half a century ago.

A very novel Christmas pageant will be held on the grounds at Prospect Park Friday afternoon by the pupils of School 14. The pageant is taken from the book written by the late Nathan B. Warren, Doctor of Music, organist and composer, who resided on the grounds which are now Prospect Park, where the temporary quarters of School 14 are now located. The idea of reviving the pageant written by the well known former Trojan came to one of the teachers of the school because the pupils of the school are now housed in the building that he once lived in. Upon investigation the teachers found a book in the Troy Pubic Library written by Mr. Warren which contained the entire program for a Christmas pageant which he gave on the old Warren estate, as some people still living will remember.

To follow the old book

The principal, Miss Anna A Morey, and the teachers of the school, who have made arrangements for the affair, plan to have their pageant exactly as outlined in the book, which is entitled "Christmas in the Olden times," the book is in three parts. The first part is the religious side of Christmas; the second part, "Christmas In the Olden Time," and the final portion deals with the bring in of the Yule log, the Boar's head ceremony and many other Christmas customs.

Old English Custom

In the preface the author explains that the idea to write the book came to him while thinking of the old baronial halls in England and he thought that he would recall those times and their picturesque Christmas affairs and customs associated with these characters in his book. The book was written for an elaborate Christmas affair which he held on his estate on Christmas. The book was published in 1866 by the A.W. Scribner Publishing Company in Mr. Warren's fifty first year of age. He died in 1899.

The Boar's Head

In this book is given the entire program for the affair, with the Christmas carols which were sung at these exercise. Prominent among these carols were:"The Norman Carol," "The First Noel," and "The Boar's Head Carol." The book was written so that the people could afterward recall what he had done on his estate. At the exercises he passed sample copies to his intimate friends. The above name carols, with the exception of "The First Noel," were written, long before the time of Mr. Warren but he rearranged them for his exercise. The celebrated Boar

Song was always sung at Christmas time and was sung at Mr. Warren's pageant, the custom originating in old England, as at that time the boar was considered a dangerous game animal and a person who killed one was doing a great and brave deed. A boar was always secured for the Christmas feast, so that the head could be brought in while the carol was chanted. At the exercise in the Warren estate a large pig's head was brought in to represent the boar.

Bringing in the Yule Log

Another of these old time customs was the brining in the Yule log, which was done by men, and every person present bared his head while it was being carried past him, which signified that all their spites and quarrels, as was troubles in the community, would be banished and brotherly love would reign amongst them. This custom was carried out at the exercise and the log was placed in the large fireplace in the Warren mansion, now the Memorial Hall at the park. At these exercises old English "waits," men who simulated those who journeyed around the country and sang these Christmas carols, sang. A large spread was set at these exercises and intimate friends were Mr. Warren's guests, although the townspeople were at the affair and witnessed the event, while some took part. The choir of the Mary Warren School also sang at these exercises, which once were carried out at the Mary Warren School. Another old Christmas custom that Mr. Warren mentions in his books is the "Mince Pie Custom," which was that in the twelve days around Christmas a person was to eat a mince pie in as many different houses as he could, but only one a day. If this was carried out it would bring good luck to the person for a month for every day that he ate a pie; that is, he ate a piece every day of the twelve he would have good luck the entire year round.

Origin of the Christmas Tree

Mr. Warren also explains the origin of the Christmas tree in his book, which he says was originated by Martin Luther, the leader of the Reformation. Since he originated the tree it has always been a custom in Christian homes that can afford it on Christmas. He also mentions the custom of kissing under the mistletoe.

The school 14 exercises

About every pupil in School 14 is to take part in the exercises on Friday, and the carrying out of many different and quaint customs have been planned for the occasion. The exercise will start at the Casino in the park, where the Shepherds and their flocks and the Three Wise men will be standing. They see the Star of Bethlehem, which will be a star falling from one of the trees, and they will journey to where they see it fall, which will be over the house known as the old Summer House in the park, which will represent the place in which our Lord was born. Upon their arrive Angels in the door will sing, "Silent Night," "Hark, the Herald Angels Sing" and" The First Noel," which was first put to muss by Mr. Warren. This will complete the first part. The second part, "Christmas in the Olden Time," will include the Christmas tree exercises at which the children will sing "The Christmas Tree" and "The Christmas Bells." A mimic tournament representing mounted Knights in the olden times will then be held, with some children acting as the Knights and others the horses. Old time games will also be played and dances given. The final act will be the bringing in of the Yule Log, the Boar's Head and the Plum Pudding. The boys will drag the large log from the Casino to the Memorial Hall, preceded by the Heralds and others carrying the Pudding and the Board's Head. The log will be placed in the huge fireplace in the hall, into which it is believe that Mr. Warren brought the Yule Log years ago. Children representing Old English Waits and the others representing Old English Mummers will sing "The Boar's Head Song," and "The Norman Carol" at these exercises which will conclude the pageant.

You can google this book and download it from Google books

1920 July 17

"Playground activities for the coming week.

Prospect Park

Monday, boy's weekly athletic tests and boys baseball, with Burden's B; Tuesday, Boys basketball with Warren's A and girls' tennis, with Burden's A; Wednesday, boys' tennis with Burden's C and girls baseball with Warrens' A; Thursday, girls volleyball, with South End, C, and girls weekly athletic tests; Friday, six boys meet equal number from Burden's A in boys weekly athletic tests, also girls; weekly athletic tests; Saturday, girls club to Prospect Museum and boys basketball, with Beman Park, C. "

1920 July 27 Troy Daily Times

"To Teach first aid work

Class at Prospect Park Museum building held up by rain – to be conducted Wednesday – Other playground events this week.

Instruction in first aid, which was to have been given at the Prospect Park Museum building Saturday afternoon, as the first if a series of classes in Home economics under the auspices of the Bureau of Recreation of the Department of Public Works, was postponed on account of rain, and will be given instead tomorrow afternoon by Miss Margaret Sheehan of the city School Nurses Corps. The members of the class will be girls enrolled at the seven municipal playgrounds organized as seven girls clubs. The second class will be held as scheduled Saturday afternoon. The courses were prepared by the Troy Women's Club, under the direction of Mrs. S Morris Pike."

1920 August 3 Troy Times

"Crowds at Playgrounds

More than five thousand children at Prospect Park during week.

Precedence in attendance at the seven municipal playgrounds during the preceding week was gained by Prospect Park. More than 5,000 children including picnic parties not enrolled at the park, played there during the week. The order of precedence among the seven parks is as follows: Prospect Park, Twelfth Street, First Street, Warren Park, South End, Burden Park and Beman Park.

The Point Contest

Warren Park leads in points. Miss Sara Holbrook, Director of Playgrounds, stated that the children at this park have shown a remarkable improvement in play as the result of organization made possible by the founding of the playground. The standing of the other parks is as follows: Twelfth Street, South End, First Street, Prospect Park, Beman Park and Burden Park. Leaders in the point contests at the various parks were: First Street, John Sullivan and John Howard, Mary Judge and Leona Veachard; Beman Park, John Shannon and Warren Arekian, Gertrude Ralson and Sothia Taskalri; Prospect Park, Loretta Kennedy and Helen Connolly, Edward Connally and William Myers; South End, James Moran and Andrew Brown, Mary Coocey and May Cooley; Warren Park, Stephen Kavanagh and William Stapleton, Helen McCrea and Ethel Kirby; Burden Park, Gregory Harian and John Burke, Sadie Walsh and Sadie Malanify; Twelfth Street, Alice Cartwright and Kenneth Haight.

Playground Graduates

Answering criticism that the playgrounds do not care for the older children, Miss Holbrook explains to day that most of the older children are employed and therefore not able to enroll at the parks. When they have their vacations, however, they report at the parks at which they have previously played, almost unanimously. Miss Holbrook point out that the reason for the overwhelming victory gained by the girls of Van Zandt, Jacobs & Co.'s baseball team over the George P. Ide & Co team, she believed was that the five of the Van Zandt, Jacobs & Co girls had been trained in baseball at Prospect Park and First Street."

1920 August 9 Troy Times

"Playground News

Tennis will be king at all of the seven municipal playgrounds during the present week, Miss Sara A Holbrook, Director of Playgrounds, announced this morning....

Care of the infants will be taken up by the girls club at the Prospect Park Museum Wednesday afternoon at 3 o'clock.......

Inter playground Contest

Miss Holbrook stated this morning that Warren Park is in the lead in the interplayground point contest. The other playgrounds in the order of their rank are as follows Twelfth Street, South End, First Street, Prospect Park, Beman Park and Burden Park.

Playground Programs

Playground activities scheduled for the present week at the seven municipal playground are as follows:

Prospect Park

Monday- Boys basketball with Burden Park C, Girls Weekly contests and tennis; Tuesday- P.R.A.A. Girls baseball with Burden Park A and tennis; Wednesday- Girls Club at museum building, boys weekly athletic contests, tennis and sewing; Thursday- Tennis, boys basketball with Twelfth Street A and unemployed juniors games; Friday – Boys baseball with South End B.P.R.A.A. Boys weekly athletic contests and tennis; Saturday- Tennis, girls volley ball with Beman Park A and boys weekly athletic contest.

1920 August 17 Troy Daily Times

Playground Standing

One hundred and First Street children are in the lead - the winners of points at the various recreation centers

Primacy in the ground points gained by the children at the seven municipal playgrounds to date has been gained by the One hundred and First Street children. The others, in the order of their standing are: Prospect Park, Warren Park, South End, One Hundred and Twelfth Street, Burden Park and Beman Park.

Individual point winners in the lead as to their respective playground: Prospect Park, Lauretta Kennedy, first and Mary Fitzgerald and Helen Connolly, tied for second place, with Edward Connolly and William Meyers in the lead among the boys......

At the Prospect Park museum tomorrow the Recreation Committee of the Troy Women's Club will conduct demonstrations of cooking for the girls clubs of the seven playgrounds. Mrs. S Morris Pike will be in charge."

1920 August 17 Troy Daily Times

"Move School 14 Class

The addition of another grade at St Francis' Parochial School will make provision for another public school class in Prospect Park building necessary.

A fifth grade will be added to the classes at St Francis' Parochial School this fall, making it necessary to remove one of the classes transferred to that institution from School 14 when the building of the latter was destroyed by fire last November. This class will probably be taken to the Warren House at Prospect Park, where classes have been conducted since the fire."

1921 July 30 Troy Daily Times

"Playground Program

Interesting Series of Activities for Youngsters at Various Parks Next week.

A fine program of activates has been prepared at the public playgrounds for next week. Girls weekly athletic contests will be held Monday at one hundred and twelfth street Park and at One Hundred and First Street Park; Tuesday at Beman Park, Prospect Park, Burden Park and South End Park Thursday at One hundred and twelfth Street Park, Warren Park, Burden Park and South End Park; Friday at Prospect Park and Warren Park and Saturday at Beman Park and Warren Park. Boys weekly athletic contests will be held Monday at Beman Park, Prospect Park, Burden Park and South End Park: Tuesday at One Hundred and Twelfth Street Park and One hundred and First Street Park; Wednesday at Beman Park, Warren Park and South End Park,. Thursday at Prospect Park; Friday One Hundred and First Street Park and Burden Park. Baseball games will be played between the boys Monday at One Hundred and Twelfth Street Park with One Hundred and First Street Park and at Warren Park with Burden.

Park Wednesday at Prospect Park with One Hundred and First Street Park Thursday at One Hundred and Twelfth Street Park with Burden Park and at Prospect Park with Beman Park. Girl's baseball games will be played Tuesday at One Hundred and First Street Park with One Hundred and Twelfth Street Park, Thurs at Beman Park with Prospect Park and at Warren Park with South End Park. Volleyball games are scheduled for Wednesday at One Hundred and Twelfth Street Park with Prospect Park, at Warren Park with Burden Park,; Thursday at One Hundred and First Street Park with South End Park and Friday at Beman Park with Warren Park. Dancing will be enjoyed at the several parks during the week. The children from each of the parks will swim at Burden Park and on Saturday will practice for the Red Cross test."

1921 August 25 Troy Times

"Playground Games

Today is "Doll Day" at Prospect Park. The park was surrendered to the little kiddies, who held a parade, each tightly clutching a doll in her arms or wheeling one before her. A sewing class exhibit will be held Saturday during the band concert.

To present Trophy

Commissioner of Public Works Morrissey will present the point Trophy cup to the winning park Tuesday afternoon. At the same time, the winners of the tennis tournament to be held at Prospect Park, Monday, will receive gold medals. The Chamber of Commerce cup will be presented to the winning baseball team Wednesday, following the deciding game.

A report on the finals of the men's and women's industrial baseball leagues was presented, and the committee gave its approval of a series of games to be held between the girls of

Lansingburgh and the girls of the southern section. The first of these games will be held Saturday September 10, at One Hundred an Tenth Street park and the second on September 17 at Prospect Park. In case each team wins of these games a third game will be played September 24 at the Center Island diamond. A game between a picked girls team and the New York Bloomer Girls will also be played on that date at Center Island."

1922 Sept 2 Troy times

"For School, 14

Announcement was made by the city educational authorities today that pending the completion of the new School, 14 building classes for the children in that district will be conducted as last year, Temporary provision will be made for the students in the Prospect Park Casino, the old Warren Mansion in the park and also at St Francis' School."

1924 March 22 Troy Times

"Report result of conference at City Hall

Superintendent of Parks Schneider recommend abolishing the foreman of laborers in the parks. Held by John M Connolly, who was asked to resign but refused stating exempt fireman and protected under civil service. He received 1300 a year plus a house to live in at Prospect Park.

Also the appointment of a park and playground commission, more police protection and guardianship for the larger playgrounds, more baseball diamonds, swimming pools etc.;

Prospect Park should have a new playground at the Hill Street entrance.

Talk that year of buying Center Island for a park and playground."

1924 August 9 Troy Times

"The program for the concert at Prospect Park tomorrow between 3 and 5 PM with Mrs. Norma Vannier Catricala, soprano, as soloist, by Dorings 105th Infantry Band, J. William Feyl, Director, will be as follows: "Gloria", from 12th Mass, Mozart; selection, "Faust," Gounod; baritone solo, "Rocked in the Cradle of the Deep," Rollinson, Evariste Roy overture, "Light Cavalry," Supple: "A Summer Evening in Hawaii," C.E. Wheeler; soprano solo, "June's The Time for Roses", E'Lorah, Mrs. Norma Vannier Catricala; waltz, "Les Sirenes," Waldteufel; sextet from "Lucia", Donisetti; "Mindin' My Business," Gus Kahn; "Gems of Stephen Foster," Laruendean; march, "Why Did I kiss That Girl," King; "The Star Spangled Banner."

Playground Report made by Supt of Playground

Miss Sara Holbrook, Superintendent of Playgrounds, made her weekly report containing activities on the grounds during the week. Ada Simmons, Alma Falls and Ellis Rosenthal are the

Directors at Prospect Park. Baseball and basketball have been the principal activity there. The boy's baseball team defeated the Van Every Park team, 7 to 1, and the Warren Park team, 22 to 9. Long and short shooting for the foul line has been the most popular game in the basketball court. Joseph Brennan is leading in scoring. A series of volleyball games resulted in Sonny's team winning from Slim's team, three of five games. James Lawlor has the tennis courts in fine shape. Charles Fausel and Victor Gilbert will represent Prospect Park in the city tennis tournament next week. The highest point winners this week were Marjorie Phillips, 429; Martha Phillips, 386, James Crosson, 339, Anthony DeLeos, 328; Howard Rail, 272."

1925 August 10 Troy Times

"Report was made at the Detective Bureau today that the restaurant conducted in Prospect Park by Austin Holian had been entered during the night and a quantity of candy, cigars and cigarettes stolen.

To present play at Prospect Park

Tomorrow evening at 6:30 o'clock a three-act play, "How One Turned His Trouble to Good Account," will be stage at Prospect Park. The cast of characters will be: Brave soldier, Harry Killfoile; drummer, Charles Wilson; rich brother, Katherine Cawfield; rich brother's son, Bertha Peck; rich brother's neighbor, Marjorie Philips; King, Sam George; Princess, Mary Ray; Pages, Frances Driscoll, Bessie Daly and Mary Considine; Archbishop, Martha Phillips,l Lord Councilor, Josephine Sharp; Command in Chief, Ed Hartley; Admiral, James Hartley; Treasurer, Frank O'Keeffe; Three Giants, Ray O'Brian, William Anderson and James Robinson; Trouble, Anna Margodian; Little Troubles, Marion Mahoney and Betty Cahill.

In between acts there will be exhibitions by the young boys and girls of Prospect Park playgrounds. This program will consist of piano and violin solos, fancy dancing and singing. George Roddy, Ruth Gibson and Margaret Bulger will be at the piano, Maurice Alpert with his violin and James Roddy will play the piano and sing. The Rohm sisters will give an exhibition in fancy dancing. Lewis First will give dances. The entertainment will be given on the west porch of the Casino."

1925 August 19 Troy Times

"Prospect Park Track Team again wins Playground Meet.

The annual track meet of the Troy playgrounds at the School 14 field yesterday was won by Prospect Park for the second year in succession. Ellis Rosenthal and Alma Falle directed the meet."

In 1926 the city created another improvement in the park. This time a brand new swimming pool designed by a relatively new pool architect and engineer Wesley Blinzt.

It was a big hit of the park until it was closed in 1994 citing costly repairs. Today it is one of only a dozen or so of 135 municipal or memorial pools designed by Wesley Bintz that he built in the United States between 1923 and the early 1960's that remain standing.

Wesley Blitz (1897-1967) was an engineer for the city of Flint Michigan and left in 1923 to start his own swimming pool construction company. Unique in design, with patents for the above ground pool design that was cheaper to build than a sunken pool. Many a baby boomer learned to swim in the pool.

1926 March 15 Daily Sentinel Rome

"$50,000 Swimming Pool in Troy Park

A municipal swimming pool in Prospect Park to cost approximately $50,000 was assured when the Board of Contract and Supply authorized preparation of plans and specifications to be presented at the next meeting of the Common Council on Thursday night. An ordinance authorizing the swimming pool was passed by the aldermen last year. The council, it is expected, will vote to advertise for bids Thursday. The Prospect Park pool is the first of an improvement program for this year estimated at a half million dollars. The paving of Congress Street is expected to be next in the line of improvements."

1926 April 29 Troy Times

"City Engineer Watts today made known the most important part of the specifications and plans for the swimming pool to be constructed in Prospect Park at a cost of $50,000. Bids for the work will be received by the Board of Contract and Supply Tuesday, May 11. The pool will be 80 by 120 feet and the overall measure 118 by 175 feet. The capacity of the pool will be 256,000 gallons. The water will be circulated steadily and it will be filtered and chlorinated while being circulated. There will be 777 lockers, and daily capacity of bathers will be 2,500. There will be 24 shower baths and on the women's side there will be 35 dressing rooms. Four springboards and 11 high diving boards will be in position. The depth of the pool will be graduated from three to nine feet. A special scum gutter will be constructed."

1926 April 29 Troy Times

"Specifications for Swimming Pool in Park; Will Cost $50,000 and Hold 256,000 Gallons of Water—There Will be 777 Lockers."

1926 June 2 Troy Times

"Among the bills audited yesterday by the Board of Contract and Supply was one of Wesley Blintz for $3,300. The bill is for services performed so far in preparing the plans for the swimming pool to be constructed in Prospect Park."

There is a plague on the pool which reads:

CITY OF TROY Harry E. Clinton, MAYOR RECREATION COMMISSION Charles F. Aldrich Mrs. M. J. Kilduff John J. Evers Dwight Marvin Mrs. B. C. Van Every Charles F. Crowley, COM. PUBLIC WORKS John C. Watts, CITY ENGINEER Arvie Eldred, SUP. SCHOOLS Sara Holbrook, SUP. RECREATION ---O--- Orr & Miller, CONTRACTORS ---O--- WESLEY BINTZ SWIMMING POOL DESIGNS Bintz Pool - Patented Lansing, Michigan --- Erected & Dedicated 1926

During the next 20 years or so the park became the center of Troy life for many Trojans. Many athletic events took place and there was an interplayground competition between all the parks for prizes through the years.

1926 August 28 Troy Times

"Athletic Meet of Playground Children Heretofore

Prospect Park was third with 26 points. Third annual track meet.

101 First Street was second. Adamsville playground in the Burg won first place. They were a newcomer only starting that year. The cup was formerly held by Prospect Park."

1927 July 15 Troy Times

"Contests at the Playgrounds

League schedules for the playground championship of the city in baseball and volleyball have been drawn up and the first league game will be played Monday.

Swimming classes are being held for the children on the playgrounds a the Prospect Park Swimming pool. Of the 38 registered to learn to swim at the Prospect Park swimming pool 15 have already learned to keep afloat and to swim a short distance after receiving five lesson.

These very definite results in teaching the youth to swim at this particular playground have been accomplished by Miss Gladys Hoffman and Miss Ruth Noyes, who are in charge of the swimming classes at that playground. Thomas H. Fitzgerald one of the life guards at the Prospect Park swimming pool, has been conducting tests for passing the senior Red Cross lifesaving requirements. Mr. Fitzgerald is a certified examiner for the American Red cross and is qualified to pass upon the merit of those trying to obtain a senior Red Cross lifesaving certificate.

James Dillon of Ida Street has ben appointed night watchmen at the Prospect Park swimming pool in place of Philip Dower, who has resigned."

1927 July 18, Troy Times

"Attendance at Playgrounds

ABOVE: Adults playing a Net game while BELOW kids play on the playground. Below image courtesy Kathy Sheehan, RCHS. The Vail Mansion (called Casino then) can be seen in the background.

Prospect Park shows an attendance of 4500 for the same park. The Prospect Park playground attendance does not include those playing tennis or the children patronized the swimming pool. There was a pet show at Prospect Park.

Total attendance for the playgrounds in the city up to last Saturday is 28,998."

1927 July 20 Troy Times

"Boat, doll and kite shows were held at Prospect and Frear Parks yesterday.

A fitting setting for the doll show was provided at Prospect Park in the form of a four room doll house built by the children and directors."

1927 July 25, Troy Times

"Park Concert

The concert given at Prospect Park yesterday by Doring's Band was delightful and the large crowd thoroughly appreciated the program. The singing of Mrs. Norma Catricalla was a feature.

Attendance at Playgrounds

Total attendance at the playgrounds during this last week was 16,500.

Prospect Park, 2,874."

1927 August 3 Troy Times

"Total attendance of the Troy Playgrounds for the week ending July 29 was 15,807. Prospect Park, with an attendance of 3,294, led the other playgrounds in attendance during the week. The feature activity was a doll, kite, and boat show held on most of the playgrounds."

1927 August 13 Troy Times

"Prospect Park is Volleyball King of Playgrounds

The Prospect Park Volleyball team won the playground chairmanship of the city in that sport yesterday afternoon by defeating Warren Park in two straight games by scores of 15-6 and 15-5. The titleholders earned the right to enter the finals by handing the 101st Street representative a similar eating the day previous. The prospect Park team showed exceptionally fine teamwork and played more as a well oiled machine rather than striving for individuality. Every man on the winning sextet scored at least once in each game."

1928 August 11, Troy Times

"The finals for the city championship in horseshoe pitching were held last night at the Prospect Park grounds. No one from Prospect Park won."

1928 August 28, Troy Times

"Last night Joe Montaine of Prospect Park failed to appear and Thomas McDermott was again winner by default."

1929 June 12 Troy Times

"Playground Attendance

Prospect Park 5,045

All playgrounds total was 17,097."

1929 August 17, Troy Times

"The annual interplayground swimming meet which took place at the municipal swimming pool at Prospect Park yesterday was won by 121st street park yesterday. Prospect Park finished second.

The meet was under the supervision of Paul J. Lynch, Recreation Director of Troy and Ellis A Rosenthal General Director of the playgrounds. More than 100 persons were entered in the meet. A large group of spectators witnessed the meet including Mayor Burns, ..."

1930 July 18 Troy Times

"Local Baseball

Russell Sage Park yesterday defeated the Frear Park nine by a 10 to 9 score and will play Prospect Park for the Central section title.

Joe Woodka's Sons of Poland team will play Dosey Doe's All Stars tonight at Prospect Park. The sons have been playing good ball this season and lost a tough game to the Insulars at Cohoes Wednesday night 6-5."

1930 August 5, Troy Times

"Prospect Park meeting held by Monitors

The speaking contest at the gathering of Troy playground Monitors held yesterday at Prospect Park was won by Betty Stufflebeam of the 101st Street playground, who will be presented an inscribe bronze medal at the closing of the park exercise.

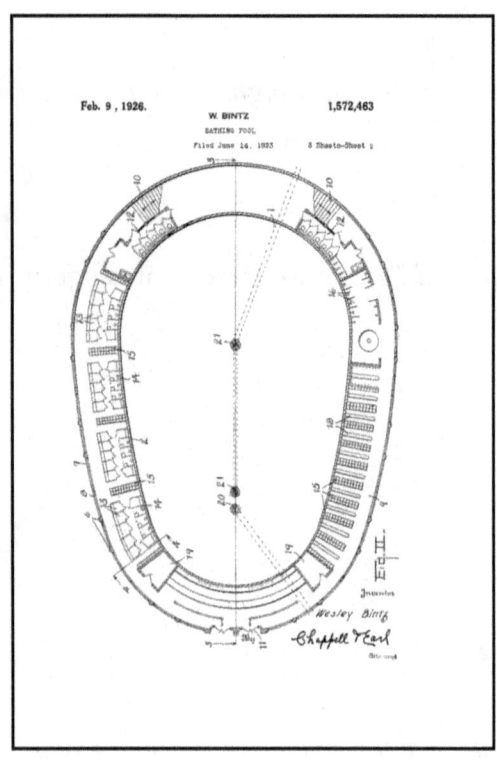

The US Patent given to Blintz on his unique above ground pools. Only a few are left in the country.

About 76 children chosen because of their interest, leadership and ability attended the monitors conclave, which was miniature convention at which representative from all the city playground were given the opportunity to learn what other playground are doing and to personal come in contact with groups from various sections of Troy. The delegate registered and were give badges.

Ellis A Rosenthal, Assistant Supervisor of Recreation, welcomed the monitors and discussed the adoption of the monitor system in the Troy playgrounds. The monitor system as it is being carried on through the playgrounds of the nation was discussed by Paul J Lynch, Supervisor of Recreation. Mr. Rosenthal was presented a Venetian vase by Rita Maloney, handcraft monitor of Burden Park, who represented the handcraft class at the park. Joseph Hormats, chairman of the Recreation Commission, also addressed the group.

Those who took part in the speaking contest won by Miss Stufflebeam, in which representatives of each playground told of the activities at his own park, were: Edward Brennan, Beman Park; Michael Dangla, Burden Park; Gabrielle Sullivan, Van Every Park; Agnes Fox, 121st Street Park; Robert Sembler, 112th Street Park; Rita Killeen, Frear Park; Ninie Whalen, Prospect Park, and Joseph Conway, Warren park.

The largest delegation present was from Van Every Park, which was represented by 12 monitors. Other delegations included: Warren, 10; Burden 9; Beman, 8: 112th Street, 8; Prospect 8; 121st Street, 6; and Frear, 3. Swimming was enjoyed after the meeting and ice cream was service the monitors. Assisting Mr. Rosenthal were Miss Catherine Broderick, George Ray and Walter Gunther. Because of the success of the conclave it is probably that

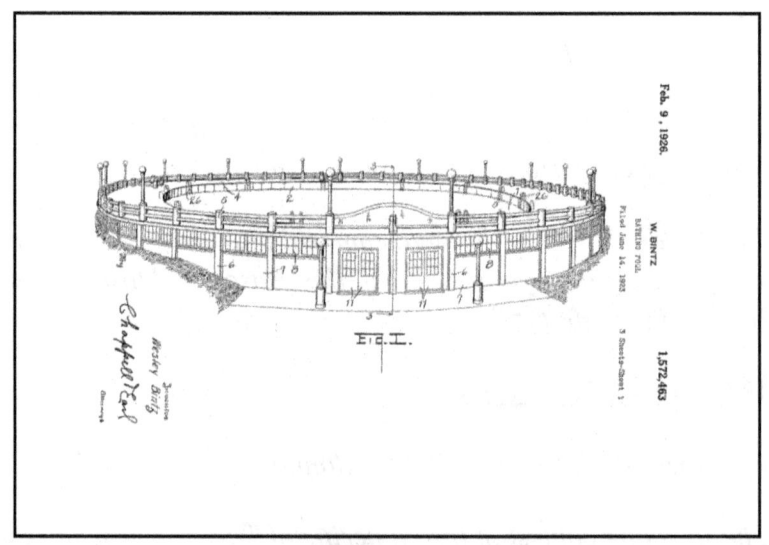

The US Patent given to Blintz on his unique above ground pools. Only a few are left in the country.

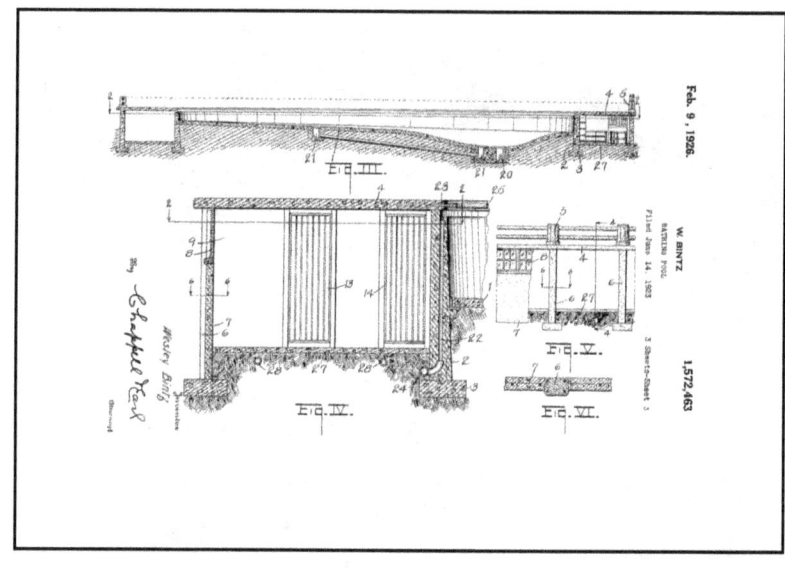

another will be held before the playgrounds close.

Pet shows are among the outstanding activities on the program of the various playground for this week. Ribbons will be awarded the winners and it is expected that several novel and unusual pets will be entered by their owners. The inter playground tennis tournament, which started at Prospect Park this morning, will end Friday evening."

1931 July 31 Troy Times

"*Monitors Hold Conference at Prospect Park*

Recreation commission sponsor conference for park leadership

The Blintz Pool waits to be restored.

Concerts and plays were popular at the bandstand and well attended.

A monitor's conference was held yesterday afternoon in Prospect Park under the auspices of the Municipal Recreation Commission, which is attempting to foster leadership among the outstanding boys and girls of the Troy playgrounds. One hundred and eight leaders who represent nine playground attendee the conference and compared their efforts, discussion much activities as teaching handicraft work, leading story telling circles, organizing games under the supervision of playground d directors and maintain discipline. One hundred and eight leaders who represent nine playground attendee the conference and compared their efforts, discussion much activities as teaching handicraft work, leading story telling circles, organizing games under the supervision of playground d directors and maintain discipline.

Ellis A Rosenthal, assistant superintendent of Recreation, received reports from each playground group. The representatives from the 12st Street playground presented a dramatization of "Red Riding Hook" during the afternoon.

Joseph Conway of Warren Park, speaking on "The benefits of a playground to a community." was the winner of an oratorical contest. In his talk he praised the work which the directors at Warren park are carrying on in spite of limited equipment. Miss Sally Lamb of Beman Park took second place, Miss Betty Garrapay of 112th Street third place and Miss Rita Mahoney of Burden Park honorable mention.

Others who took part in he contest were Donald Maley of 123rd street, Miss Anna Waters of 101st. Street, Spencer Rogers of Frear Park, Miss Mary King of Van Every Park, and Joseph Carelli of Prospect Park, who sand a solo. The judges for the contest were Joseph J. Hormats, chairman of the Recreation Commission, and Miss Julia M., Ryan.

Refreshments were served during the afternoon and a grab bag was enjoyed, with awards furnished by the Commission. Later the monitors enjoyed swimming in eh park pool. Another conference is being planned for August by the Committee in charge, which is composed of Paul J Lynch, Honorary Chairmen; Ellis A Rosenthal, Chairmen, and Miss Katherine Broderick, Miss Janet Coffeen, Miss Marion Dunn, Miss Elizabeth Bailey, Miss Kay Lasher, Miss Mary Burkey, George Thompson ad James O'Brien, all park directors.

The various playgrounds were represent by the following monitors:

Burden Park- Mary Piskitz, Frances Keith, Mae Murphy, Rita Maloney, Genevieve Koski, Frances Stackura, Raymond Yannick, John Dorrick and Helen Rado.

123rd Street – Harold Palmer, William Grund, James Fox, Lynwood Rubie, Michael Tague, Arnold Mealy, Margaret Walker, Frances Fox, Martha Hansen, Helen Hansen, Irving Warren, Donald Fisher, Anna Carner and Donald Mealy.

112th Street – Carl Andersen, Betty Gavitt, Andrew Rokier, Mary Cooney, Helen Daviddeo, James Broderick, Muriel Prefore, Jean Prefore, Ned Kelleher, James Nelson, Berry Garrapay,

August Kokfer, Francis Kokfer, Roy LeBeau, Lillian Kaiser, Rita Kaiser, Muriel Caren, Ruth Rafferty and Thelma Marco

110th Street – Agnes Meighan, Anne Broderick, Louise hall, Margaret Plante, Anne Waters, Eleanor Waters, Clara Hall, Rosemary Waters, Ned Murphy and Henry Maslott.

Frear Park – Mary McGrath, Lois Van Every, Clara O'Bryan, Dorothy Ostrander, Stewart Campbell, Gertrude Ostrander, Bernice Bianchette, Ed Doherty, Jack Kennedy, Spencer Rogers, Frances Connors, Arthur Mathasie, Donald Ostrander, John McGrath, Joseph Eissbleum, Joseph Garrett, Harry Garrett, Charles Snyder, and Betty Finn.

Beman Park – Sally Lamb, Bobby Lamb, Nancy Walsh and Jean Schleich.

Prospect Park – Monny Rosenthal, Tony Paul, Eugene Richmond, Mary Korkemas, Louis Staley, Jerry Marchese, Joseph Agostine, Sam Corelli, Jose Corelli, Red Corelli, Russell Corelli and Louise Steringer.

Warren Park – Robert McGrane, Tony Dreno, Mary Conway, Rose Stadnick, James Ryan, Paul Doody, Pat Derenzo, Mary Feluta, Stephen Barnock, Joseph Conway, Dora Duffy, and Rose Paslowksi.

Van Every Park - Mary Lucosky, Carolyn Zalacky, Bertha Zalacky, Mary King, Anna May, William Seap, Joseph Seap, Jack O'Brien, and Jack Murphy."

1931 August 8 , Troy Times

"Interplayground meet held last night in Prospect Park

The Warren Park swimmers won first place last night in the eight annual inter playground swimming meet held at the municipal pool in Prospect Park. Victory came to the South Trojans only a after a stirring duel with the Prospect Park representations, champions of last years meet. The final score Gave Warren Park 41 points and Prospect Park 37 points.

The matches began last night at 8:30 o'clock and continue until well after dark. This was the first year the meet was held at night and officials expressed satisfaction with the increased attendance which the night event drew.

The pool itself presented a gala aspect for the annual event, decked in flags and buntings made by the handicraft classes in the various playgrounds. AS duck came on and the powerful lights were tuned on the pool, the scene became even more attraction.

Horseshoe Finals

Semifinals in the horseshoe pitching contests will be stage in all the playgrounds tomorrow afternoon and evening and the finals in this sport will be run off on Friday night at Prospect Park.

The recreation commission has announced that the municipal pool at prospect park has been open and will be open for the remainder of the season."

A view of the fountain, the band stand and Vail Mansion in the background.

Same view today.

Much of the popularity with adults was the fountain area surrounded by many beds of flowers.

1931 August 20 Troy Times

"Program presented at Prospect Park

Miss Janet Coffeen, Miss Marion Dunne, Harry Bartle, and George Ray, directors at Prospect Park, were in charge of the weekly entertainment program presented last evening by the children of the playground. Songs and dances were presented by Ronald Ward, Marjorie Perreault, Ruth Moieller, Jean Doney, Marjorie Harrison, Francis Conde, and James Harley, with George Ray acting as announcer, E. Wood of Warren Park , first; M Stewart of Prospect Park, second, and k. Ostrander of Frear Park, third, have been announced by the Recreation Commission as winners of the 40 yards free style swim in the Class B division of last weeks inter playground swimming meet at Prospect Park."

1932 July 19 Troy Times

"Troy playground season promises to be banner one.

Attendance thus far breaks marks of last year, recreation commissioner announces.

With an attendance total, exclusive of Saturday and Sunday, of 33,068 from July 5 to July 15 Troy playgrounds seem pointed for a similar period last year, which included three days more than that covered by the present report, was 28,719.

Prospect Park has 4804.

Recreation commissioner Lynch's report on the playground activities continues as follows:

"The lack of funds on the part of the general public is also showing a reaction in the handcraft activities. Not only children but their mothers, older sister and brothers are taking an active part in handcraft activity for the most part making utilitarian articles. The weaving of belts from both cellophane and fiber is being done by both boys and girls. The leading handcraft activity of this season is crocheting. Our entire supply of material for crocheting which we thoroughly would last for the season is all gone with one week. The people using this material pay us what the material costs us. They can crochet a beret at a cost of give centers because we buy the material in bulk.

The total attendance of the swimming pool to date has been 17,582 of where there were 647adults, 8845 children and 8090 free swims."

1932 September 1, 1932

Prospect Park Honors Mother of Playgrounds

Mrs. Frank W. Thomas Greeted By Children at Closing Exercises of Season

Mrs. Frank W. Thomas Greeted By Children at Closing Exercises of Season Twenty-six years ago Mrs. Frank W. Thomas invited several women's club Presidents of the city to meet with her

Postcard views of the fountain area during its heyday. The foundation is still there partially buried.

at her home on Collins Avenue and discuss plans for setting apart certain places of the city for children's playgrounds. The direct outgrowth of that meeting was the formation of the Prospect Park playground, and the indirect outgrowth was the development of our present highly organized welfare and recreational work among the city playgrounds and parks.

Last evening Mrs. Thomas drove up to Prospect Park to view the closing exercises at the Prospect playground. As she was quietly enjoying the entertainment Paul J. Lynch, Supervisor of Recreation, spied her and after greeting her announced to the children that "the mother of playgrounds" was with them. The youngsters, many of whose parents had been directed by Mrs. Thomas in their playground activities, came forward eagerly to shake hands with her and meet her personally.

All the equipment and apparatus for Prospect Park were planned by Mrs. Thomas, who founded the park March 6, 1906. She was elected President of the Women's Improvement Society, which was planned to supervise the playgrounds, and served as its active and honorary head for six years. During that time she went to the park each morning to direct the activities of the children.

The round-about path leading to the playground at the park made it difficult for mothers and children to enjoy the playground comforts. Fighting against those who believed that a stairway would spoil the landscape garden scheme of the park, Mrs. Thomas finally succeeded in having the city build a convenient staircase. She won the lasting gratitude of all the Prospect Park mothers and the stairway is still called in her honor, the Carrie Thomas stairway. Mrs. Thomas also collected the money and purchased apparatus for the Van Every playground, two years after the Prospect Park one was started.

Troy was outstanding in the early development of the nation's playgrounds and Mrs. Thomas was chosen as the most progressive woman of this section in the playground movement and served as the Northern New York playground representative. She still prizes an autographed framed portrait of Theodore Roosevelt, which he sent to her.

Last night's entertainment was in the form of a vaudeville program which about 2,000 persons attended. George Ray, park director, acted as master of ceremonies, and was assisted by Miss Janet Coffeen and Harry Bartle, who are also directors at the park.

The program included a song, "Whistle and Blow Your Blues Away," by Gloria Jane Scofield; "My Mother's Eyes," sung by Sol Samiof; songs by B. Griffin, Letty McHugh, Rose McHugh and Mary Frazier; a dance by Roland Ward; an interpretation of "St. Louis Blues," by Marian Dunn; tap dancing by Curley Fisher, and numbers by Margaret Fiske, Mary Frances Stewart and Betty McMahon.

1933 Dec 30, Albany Evening News

Trojans woke up at the end of 1933 and were alarmed to read that the Warren Mansion was going to be torn down. Harry Penny from Cohoes wrote a letter to the editor of the Albany Evening News:

Preserve Manor House

To the Editor of the Albany Evening News

Read your article, "One of Oldest Troy Homes to be Razed," and am taking the liberty of submitting the following item in the protest of the demolition of this old landmark, hoping that you can give the protest a space in your alert publication.

"Something for Troy to Be Proud Of?" - Relative to CWA force tearing down the Warren Manor, Prospect Park, Troy. My recollection is that the property and manor were given to the city of Troy. Now, the tinsel and fancy wrappings being departed that is gone, the gift become shabby from neglect in painting it, etc. it goes to the ash heap - or where does the material go?

It would seem that Prospect Park is large enough without destroying the manor for the small plot of land on which it stands. Though it is easier to destroy than to create or rebuilt it is quite possible that the CWA workers would have as much employment or more in fixing up the old manor house than in its destruction and surely, a city that size of Troy ought to be in a position to buy such material as is needed to repair this ancient landmark, the last of its kind in this vicinity. The demolition of this structure is an irreparable loss.

Henry Penney

Cohoes, Dec 27, 1933

Ironic that the destruction of this important historic site was a project of the Civil Works Administration of the 1930s during the Great Depression. It was replaced by the WPA due to much controversy. Ironic in that another WPA project was the HABS program that sent unemployed architects around the country documenting these kinds of historic buildings. Sadly, this Alexanderson Jackson Davis designed mansion was not included. The CWA laid over 12 million feet of sewers, improved or built 255,000 miles of roads, 40,000 schools and almost 4,000 playgrounds. They also built 250,000 outhouses.

1934 July 9 Troy Times

"The English Third Order benefit for St. Anthony's Church which was previously schedule for June 14, will be held Wednesday evening at Prospect Park Casino. Card and dancing will be enjoyed and wards will be made. The casino will be open at 7 o'clock."

1940 January 12, Troy Times

"Group considers ways of making "City Beautiful."

The young Married People's Group of the Fifth Avenue State Street Methodist Church met last evening and discussed "What to do to Beautify the City."

Many suggestions were made such as : improvement of Prospect Park by planting shrubs and flowers as was at one time done; erecting a band stand for public concerts and restoring the Vail House, ..."

1940 August 13 Troy Times

"Summer nights dancing for boys and girls.

The year 1943 marked an end to an important part of the park's history when the old Vail House, known as the Casino, burned to the ground. The Warren Mansion had already been torn down and the burning of the Vail House was the last remnant of an earlier history of some of the early movers and shakers of the founding of Troy.

1943 February 22, Knickerbock News

"Park Casino Burns

Prospect Park Casino, one of Troy's landmarks, is in ashes today after a fire Saturday night. Cause of the fire is not known. The structure had been condemned as unsafe and had not been used except for storage. The large frame structure cost $35,000 when built."

1943 Feb 23, Times Record

"Fire Razes Casino, City Landmark at Prospect Park

Unoccupied building, used for storage, covered by insurance; water lines cripple traffic.

A spectacular fire that cast a reflection visible from miles Saturday night wrecked the Prospect Park Casino, one of the city's landmarks. The cause of the blaze was not determined.

The building had not been occupied for some time and officials were unable to advance any theory as to the cause of the fire. The structure had been condemned and unsafe and had not been used other than for storage purposes. It was owned by the city and covered by insurance.

According to officials, the large frame building with intersected brick partitions cost about $35,000 to erect. It was used partially at one time for residential purposes by the late John Connolly, who was superintendent of Troy's park system for many years and still alter by Mrs. Anthony Stehle and Mrs. Joseph Mullen, who served as matrons at the park.

Park Grounds purchased

The building was one of two large residential structures which were on the land when it was purchased by the city from the Warren family for $110.000 in February 1903.

One of the buildings was used as the Casino and the other building situated on the western side of the park overlooking the brow of the hill was used as a museum for Troy historical relics for many years.

This latter building was torn down a number of years ago. For a time its site was considered as a site for a new high school building. Authorization for the purchase of the park grounds was given in an act passed by the legislature and sponsored by Assemblyman John F. Ahern. The park was laid out by Garnet D. Baltimore, local landscape engineer.

Despite the hazardous condition of the park highways caused by ice, hundreds of persons went to the scene. Considerable difficulty was experienced by firemen who were compelled to lay a line first from Congress and Christie Streets and later from the rear of St Francis de Sales Church, along the winding road to the Casino. The hose used by the firefighters was sufficient to cover several city blocks. Laying of a line from Congress and Christie Streets crippled traffic considerably. Bus patrons were forced to leave the buses west of Christie Street and board other busses above the church. Three pumpers were used to relay the pressure along the one line laid from the rear of the church.

Playground Equipment Safe

Many person who will depend on the city parks for recreation next summer, now that gasoline rationing has become so stringent, wondered today just how much of the park equipment stored in the building was destroyed.

For the assurance of the children Recreation Commissioner Edward Wachter announced that all the swings, slides and other playground equipment used by the juvenile patrons of the park was stored in the swimming pool building and so was not harmed.

Public Works Commissioner Thomas F.

The Thomas staircase is still there but the playground that it led to is long gone. Replaced by seven tennis courts, a handball court, and basketball court.

FitzGerald said that about 75 park benches were saved from the fire and that about fifty or sixty were destroyed or damaged.

Many of the destroyed ones may be rebuilt by salvaging the iron parts, Mr. Fitzgerald stated.

Most of the lawn mowers and tools were also saved.

Many citizens were concerned about the loss of equipment realizing that with war conditions, it would be virtually impossible to replace any of it."

The Beginning of Decline of Prospect Park

During the 1940's the park was beginning to show signs of neglect. It was also the beginning of the decline of Troy as an industrial powerhouse and people began flocking to the suburbs, industries moved south, and the ill conceived federal Urban Renewal and DOT I-797 fiasco took its toll on the city. Baby boomers such as the author were the last to enjoy the park in any form using the pool, playground and athletic events, many sponsored by the Troy Boys Club.

Perhaps the most telling story of the demise of the park was written by "Ida Hill" in a letter to the editor in response to a Pulse of the People item in the Troy Times Record on August 26, 1953:

"Pulse of the People

Prospect Park

Editor The Record. About ten days ago I noticed an article in the Pulse of the People signed with the pseudonym "Taxpayer," relative to the condition of Prospect Park and commenting particular on its alleged improvement within the last ten years. Apparently "Taxpayer" has not been a resident of Troy for too many years or, if so, had not made many trips to this park prior to the last ten years. I am a native of Troy, having been born in and lived all of my life in the section near the park, and I feel that the park is in a deplorable condition when compared with its beauty of former years. It has been on the downgrade since the 1920s.

You will perhaps recall the beautiful rustic fences and the many flower beds which were all through the park grounds. There was a large round bed of flowers at the main entrance on Congress Street which was usually planted with colorful tulips in the spring, and cannas, salvia, etc., in the summer and fall. There was also a similar bed on a mound just east of the stairway which leads to the playground and another one in the plat west of the Vail House. There was also a large rose garden at the head of the main entrance road.

There were two or three large flag poles at various points in the park which have been removed and never replaced. One of these was located at the extreme Southwest end of the park which overlooks South Troy, and there was a Civil War cannon near it, as well as beds of flowers. I

"The Cottage" was the nickname for the Nathan B. Warren mansion designed by Alexander Jackson Davis. Used as a city museum and later as School 14. Torn down by the city as a public works project in the 1930s.

"The Terrace" as it was called where Vail's Road intersected with Warren's Road. The mansion is to the right.

Warren Road today. The mansion was to the right and the steps going down to Cottage or Vail's Road is to the left where I am standing taking the photo.

believe this is the only location in the park today where there is a flag pole, and of course, the cannon has long sing disappeared. Also, there are very few benches left in the park.

There was a large wooden bandstand on a mound adjoining the west end of the playground. Usually band concerts were presented at this point on Sunday afternoon in the summer months. There was a lane or road running downhill from this bandstand which I believe was called "The Mall." At about the center point of this road was a large ornamental fountain set in concrete which was bordered with a round plat of grass. Each of the four sides of this plat contained a small bed of flowers, each being a different shape. While I may not be entirely accurate, I believe one was diamond shaped, one a cross, one a crescent and one star shape. On both sides of "The Mall." and on another lane which ran from north to south from the south end of the fountain there were beds of tulips on each side in the spring which were replaced with geraniums, begonias and other summer and fall flowers as the growing season progressed.

A tall rustic summer house was at the extreme west end of the park and there was also a beautiful memorial drinking foundation in this immediate vicinity. There was also a smaller summer or lookout house on the south end of the park near the road which leads down to Hill Street. This road has been in very poor condition for several years and now is impassable due to the fact that barricade have been placed across it at least on the upper end.

The steps from Warren Road leading to the Warren Mansion that was once in front of these stairs. The City demolished it in the 1930s. This is also where Ebenezer Wilson, Uncle Sam's brother had his farm.

The park contained two old mansions (the Warren House at the northwest end of the park and the Vail House on a plat of ground adjoining the tennis courts). There was a caretaker at the Warren house, and I believe the park superintendent or other responsible city employees usually had living quarters on the second floor of the Vail House. There was also a confectionery store on the ground floor of this Vail House, and refreshments were served at tables on the large porch of this house. The building contained rest rooms on the first floor as well as other rooms which were used for storage of certain movable playground equipment, and by playground instructors and children on rainy days.

You may recall that there was once a nice artificial lake on the hill directly west of the baseball diamond. At the west end of this lake (I believe the source through pipes) was a very pretty rustic bridge which was slightly arched and contained a platform which was reached by a few stops on each side. Also there was a rustic boathouse on the inside shore of the lake. Children skated on this lake during the winter months in fact, many of Troy's children learned to skate there.

As children we were taught to appreciate the beauty of such surroundings and especially while we were attending school at the park buildings. Old School 14 was burned on election night in 1919, and subsequently the four upper grades and the principal's office of this grammar school were housed at the park buildings, the fifth and sixth grades and the principal's office at the Vail House, and the seventh and eight grades at the Warren House. We were forbidden to walk on the grass or to damage shrubbery, and anyone who dared to violate these rules was punished.

Prior to its occupancy for school purposes part of the first floor of the Warren House was used a museum for military relics. Another part of the first floor thereof was used for storage of maintenance equipment. I believe the second floor was occupied by the caretaker. This beautiful old home was later torn down. I vaguely recall hearing something to the effect that it had become over run with rodents. Couldn't such a situation have been corrected and the lovely building restored and preserved as a museum?

In the days of our youth there was a force of special foot patrolmen assigned to the park. They were certainly very efficient and seemed to be personally interested in keeping down acts of vandalism as well as protecting children. We all highly respected these men and they had our interests at heart. If such as plan were in effect today perhaps there would be a few more whole globes on the electric lights in the park.

What Troy really needs is to acquire some civic pride and restore some of the old time beauty to Prospect Park, erect a modern superintendents or caretakers resident therein, have an adequate and competent maintenance force assigned there, and a sufficient force of adequately paid foot patrolmen on duty who would have access to city police call boxes and telephones in case of emergencies. Suggested police coverage would be from mid morning until midnight or 1 AM in the warm months especially.

Ida Hill

Troy"

Finally in 1963, Troy was recognizing the almost 40 years of service given by the city's recreation department citing almost 300,000 children benefiting from its various programs.

1963 July 6 Times Record

Troy's recreation program comes far after 39 years of service to children.

In 1963 152,000 children participated in activities at the city's 21 playgrounds. Overall 298,560 children and teenagers participate in its program and athletic leagues.

During its first year of organized supervision, 1924, Troy had six play sites: Prospect Park, Beman Park, Van Every Park, Warren Park, 101st Park and 112th Street.

Miss Sarah Holbrook was the fist superintendent.

In 1963 Prospect Park swimming pool brought in $1,118.75.

21,000 persons patronized the 12 clay tennis courts. [There are now 14 tennis courts]

Prospect Park skating area would replace Belden's Pond as major skating site."

Chapter Five
The Future of Prospect Park

For over a century, Prospect Park served as an outdoor venue for thousands of Trojans. It has seen good and bad days but it has been long enough to sit idly by and do nothing about it. Troy has been undergoing an on-again, off-again, on again, Renaissance of sorts over the last few years. Many younger people are moving into the city - with families - and it is time to bring Prospect Park back to its former glorious condition. You have read in the last four chapters the complete history of Mount Ida and its evolution into Troy's premier park. So now it's time to roll up the sleeves, put on the thinking caps, and together polish up this jewel and bring it back to full capacity. While Albany and Schenectady have been doing an excellent job of upkeep on their main public parks, Troy has fallen behind in the offerings that Albany and Schenectady residents take for granted. Why should Trojans expect less? Albany's Washington Park enjoys thousands of visitors during their annual Tulip Fest and Christmas lights drive through. The park's playhouse has many excellent theatrical performances each year. Schenectady's Central Park has boat rentals on their lake, a band shell, a casino where you buy refreshments, and a good size playground and pool for the kids. However one must consider whether the park in Troy is a priority considering problems facing the city: it does not have a city hall, its public library may be closing or moving, an annual parade that has been a tradition for years was cancelled, massive financial problems in which the State of New York is getting involved, infrastructure problems, abandoned buildings, and a newspaper barely hanging on. Fixing the park may be on the bottom of the list.

Today the swimming pool has grass and trees growing in it. The area of the former lake has a pavilion where people can have small gatherings. The service roads are passable but could use some work. The hillside is not mowed anymore so there are few places where one can get a grand view of the Hudson Valley like in former times. The fountain and drinking fountain are gone. The fountain area has its circular base intact though the pool area is mostly filled in. There is a small flagpole and small monument in honor of Francis Brown, killed in the infamous USS Liberty attack in 1967. The grand Warren Mansion is now a flat concrete area with a spray in the middle to cool off kids. The grand mall has the playground in it though only a few play items like a swing and even the whirly-go-round seems to be the same one the author used when he a preteen. The tennis courts seem to be kept up, and hand ball court goes unused. The roads that comprise the northern part of the park are closed off. A cheaply made Uncle Sam pavilion sits where the former observation tower was located. All other former access roads with the exception of the one at Congress Street are barely visible. The western slope of the park which intersects with the former Ferry Street is a virtual Hoverville, signs of homeless encampments everywhere.

In 1943, Garnet D. Baltimore, who designed the park wrote about the neglect of the park that he designed 34 years earlier:

"Editor The Record: The other day, while driving decline through the country with a middle-aged couple of acquaintances, the conversation reverted to Prospect Park. The lady remarked that some of the happiest days of their courtship were spent in the park.

"In these days it was a beautiful spot. The flowers, the trees, the lawns, the views and oftentimes the music would lend its charm to our enjoyment. But today every official element of beauty has been destroyed or removed. The Warren mansion, that unique structure (which could easily have been restored with WPA funds) was torn down at the whim of an iconoclast; the Vail mansion burned by vandals; the Bascom fountain, donated to the park by the generosity of Mrs. Bascom, dismantled and removed; the band stand eliminated; the paths neglected and overgrown with grass. Not a comfort station in all the broad area.

"Is the civic pride of Trojans so deadened that no murmur of regret is heard at this willful neglect?

"Let us, however, take heart and hope that the incoming administration will restore these neglected areas to their pristine beauty, and curb the vandalism by strict police supervision so that respectable citizens can again enjoy in peace the comfort their rightful heritage.

"GARNET D. BALTIMORE

"Troy, Nov. 16, 1943."

Baltimore, Garnet D. "Pulse of the People: Alas Poor Yorick!" Times Record [Troy, NY]. November 22, 1943: 12.

Let's take a look at what needs to be done.

The Pool

The pool should to be brought back to working condition. Grants, Community Development Block Grants (CDBG), and other forms of financial assistance must be obtained. First a cost estimate for repairs should be taken and it can be done in stages. The weeds need to be removed from the deep end of the pool since their roots can cause serious damage, if they haven't already. Any cracks should be temporarily filled to slow further deterioration. In 2015, it was announced that the Bintz pool in Tampa Florida was undergoing a $1.8 million restoration - the only other one in

Prospect Park police patrol in 1948. Officers (left to right) Vince Cunningham, Bill Sheeran, and Pete Magneto, with patrol car TPD 2.

Originally Philip Heartt, then Albert Heartt lived here until Henry Vail purchased it. His nephew David was the last private owner.

The site of the former Vail Mansion.

View of upper Congress Street and Ferry Street from Mount Ida. Troy Seminary (Four Towers) can be seen on the other side of the original limits of Mount Ida.

existence. If it cannot be brought back as a pool, another use should be developed, perhaps a restaurant, small performance center, or skating rink.

The Gatehouse

The Warren Gatehouse needs to be brought back to the upper Congress Street location and serve as the park visitor center. A park ranger can live there on the second floor and attend to the park. The gatehouse can also serve as a visitor's center for the whole city and can be the location where you rent skis and skates during winter. It's time to open the park up during winter time. The former lake should be excavated just deep enough to form a shallow basin that can be filled with water for skating during the winter. This park is the only one in the Capital District without a water body. The gatehouse has had some interesting history at its current location. In 1971 it was the "Monolith House," home for several members of a local rock band and shortly after that was the residence of this author for a couple of years shortly being married. His rock band, Horton Strong, practiced in the basement. There have been some estimates over the years to restore it with the last one in 2001 estimated at over $300,000 which seemed high. The author obtained a quote of $30,000 to move it back to the park location in the late 1980s.

Winter Access

Even Garnet Baltimore complained that the park was not open during winter. Albany and Schenectady have their parks open. There is no logical reason why Prospect Park is closed. It is true that the topography may prevent automobile access but hiking, skating, cross country

The wooden observation tower allowed a view of about 25 miles of the Hudson River Valley.

The northern part of the park from the air. Way too many tennis courts. Google Earth.

Observation Tower

A new metal fire proof observation tower should be built where the old one was located in the area where the TROY stone blocks are located. The surrounding hillside underbrush and weed trees should be trimmed or removed to allow the original 25 mile view to be returned.

skiing should be allowed.

Roads and Trails and Playgrounds

The road that hugs the northern part of the park should be reopened but not for cars. The asphalt taken up and gravel put down as in the original design. Driving should only be allowed to the pavilion, tennis courts and picnic areas. The rest of the park should be for foot traffic only. Trails should be reopened down the western side of the hill. A new modern playground should be built but it should be placed where the original one was closer to the tennis courts. Half of those tennis courts should be removed. This would reopen the former "mall" area. The handball court should be removed. Basketball courts need to be refurbished. Fourteen tennis courts? Really? Is that many needed? How about four? Rustic fences should be brought back. Recreational pursuits change so a needs assessment would in order.

Education

There should be a bio blitz (complete inventory of plants and animals) done and a field guide to the park created and made available to the public. Create an experimental farm and grow some

1909 Aerial view of Troy from Mount Ida, now Prospect Park. Many of the buildings you see at the bottom are gone. Images taken by Haines Photo Co.

of the early fruit trees such as the Ida Green Gage Plum. Cornel Cooperative Extension could be an asset here.

Lighting and Safety

Historic period poles should be placed along the gravel walkways. Security cameras should be placed throughout the park to keep down vandalism and crime. Cameras have worked very well in Vale Cemetery in Schenectady, monitored by police. An earlier light pole is still near the fountain area though being overtaken and hidden by trees.

Beautification

Bring back the circular fountain and beds of flowers and shrubs. There are garden clubs throughout the area and certainly a volunteer group can be found to tend to them. Schenectady's Central Park has an award winning Rose Garden run by volunteers. Albany has an award winning Tulip garden. It would also be appropriate to bring back some of former flowers that were cultivated by Heartt, Vail, and Warren in a memorial garden there.

Band Shell

A new band shell performance area should be built along the area of the former site near the old Vail Mansion. Both Albany and Schenectady have one and provide entertainment. Fireworks should once again take place during the 4th of July from the hill.

Mt. Ida from Troy Seminary (RPI). Much of the homes seen are gone. From stereo taken by Charles F. Himes collection, c. 1860-70.

Restore Cemetery

As you read in some of Garnet Baltimore's annual reports, the old Mt. Ida Cemetery (not the one on Pawling Avenue) was considered part of the park and as late as 1966 was shown on a map published in the Troy newspaper to be an integral part of the park. This cemetery has taken a beating by the city as has the other Mt. Ida cemeteries. Many of Troy's early citizens and soldiers were buried there including Asa Anthony, whose house fire instigated the beginning of Troy's fire department; Susan Heartt, wife of Albert P. Heartt; Captain Benjamin Mann who served at Bunker Hill; and Sarah Vanderheyden, daughter of Mathias one of the founders of Troy.

The original Mt Ida Cemetery was given to

the city, then village of Troy, in 1814 by Stephen Van Rensselaer, the Great Patroon. The first person buried there was George Young who died on November 6, 1814, who was 55 years old.

It was fenced off and had labeled roads through the cemetery however the graves were supposedly dug up and brought to Oakwood Cemetery but there is some controversy over that. In the 1864 (March 5) Daily Times it reported that:

"Every day there is a collection of two or three hundred lads in the old burying – ground on Ida Hill. They indulge in fights, mutilate the tomb--stones and desecrate the graves. This should be stopped."

The cemetery is now a dumping ground for all kinds of what appears to be private material.

Mt. Ida from Troy Seminary (RPI). Warren Mansion can be seen on top of Ida. From stereo taken by Charles F. Himes collection, c. 1860-70.

With Troy University in the background, Edwin Emerson took a selfie on Mount Ida near the Warren Mansion on May 7, 1862.

Fencing

Rustic fences like the ones that were there should be returned instead of those ugly metal roadside bumpers from the 1960s.

Police Patrol

A horse patrol during the day would be appropriate. Security cameras should be placed around the park by not only the police but by the interested public via the Internet.

Dismantle the Uncle Sam Pavilion

The Uncle Sam Pavilion located where the observation tower use to be needs to be dismantled. It is poorly constructed and suffers from neglect.

Relaxing in the park was a daily ritual for many Trojans during the first half of the 20th century. The observation tower was a popular attraction until it was burned.

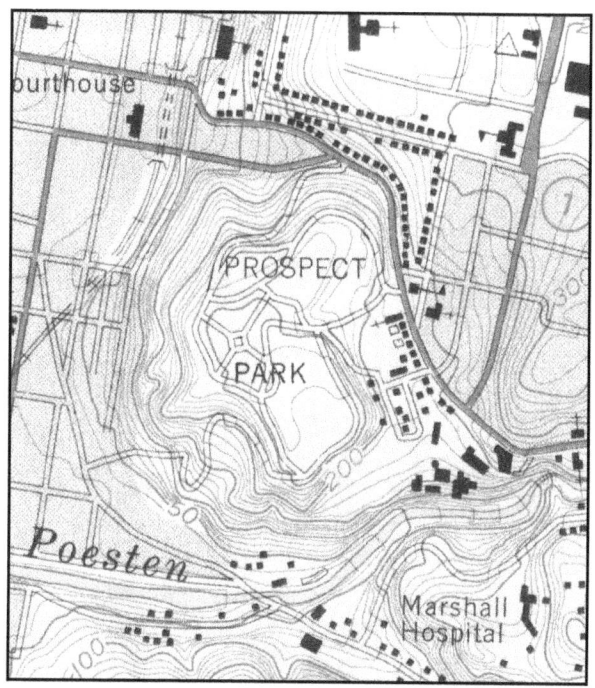

1953 Topo map showing the original road and trail system before most were abandoned.

Carriage Rides

During the summer there should be carriage rides and during winter, when snow, sleigh rides. There could be a special Prospect Park day with carriage rides, music, dance and other performances.

The park should be open all year round. Closing during the winter has been a controversy since it opened.

The cemetery needs to be cleaned out and brought back to being part of the park. It would be a great area for exploration as it is right next to the Poestenkill.

Connect Mt. Ida Falls

For most of Troy's existence, Mt. Ida falls served not only as an early industrial base but

The old Mt Ida Cemetery at the base of the hill off Walnut Street in 1904.

as parkland as well with an wooden and wrought iron bridge crossing near the falls. In the 1970s, fill from a nearby development was dumped in part of the ravine so that lazy visitors could park their car and not have to get out to see the falls. With Federal grants, trails and rails were built and an observation deck that was quickly put to the torch by typical hooligans. The park was closed off because some ill thinking person decided to dive off and hurt himself so the city decided to punish the rest of the population. This however has not stopped accidental

Photograph from Mount Ida showing extensive number of headstones in old cemetery.

Upper part of Mt. Ida Falls.

deaths. In June, 2016, a 16 year old boy died when he fell about 20 feet hitting his head before entering the water. Closing off the park to the entire public who could enjoy the park because of these periodic deaths is not logical.

This part of the park needs to be redeveloped and to connect via trails to the main park.

There will be those that say none of this can be done because it costs money. That's just an excuse for not wanting to do anything. There are plenty of Trojans who will come together to make it happen.

Teddy Roosevelt said it well: *"The nation behaves well if it treats its natural resources as assets which it must turn over to the next generation increased, and not impaired, in value."*

Sources

Most of the research for this book came from early newspaper accounts from the Times Record, Knickerbocker News, Troy Times, Albany Evening News, Daily Sentinel Rome, Troy Daily Times, Brooklyn Eagle and Troy City Annual Reports, Troy Department of Public Works Annual Report, Troy Public Improvement Commission Annual Report, Troy Public Library Map Room, Troy Room, Troy North Quadrangle, New York, Rensselaer Polytechnic Institute, Troy, NY, LaFleur, Robert G., 1963-05, Glacial Geology Of The Troy, N.Y., Quadrangle. Robert G. LaFleur. Albany, NY: New York State Museum, 1965, and Christopher Philippo.

Mt. Ida Falls needs to be connected to Prospect Park as it once was. This photo was taken in October, 1861.

Print from steel engraving titled **Chute d'eau pres le Mont Ida** - *Waterfall near Mount Ida*. First edition of Jean B.G. Roux de Rochelle's *Etats-Unis d'Amérique*. Paris: Firmin Didot Freres, [1837]. Bottom: Civil engineering students from Rennselaer Polytechnic Institute in 1888 using the area for educational purposes. Courtesy RPI Archives.

The Griswold Wire Works during the 19th and early 20th centuries utilized power from the Mt. Ida Falls directing the powerful falls down sluice ways and powering turbines located in the buildings.

Three examples of barbed wire produced at the Griswold Wire Works. Courtesy Glade Wasden.

www.ingramcontent.com/pod-product-compliance
Lightning Source LLC
Chambersburg PA
CBHW080341170426
43194CB00014B/2642